Hiding Under the Table

by

Dennis Henning

with Patricia Woods

Americana Publishing
Albuquerque, New Mexico, U.S.A.
2004

Americana Publishing, Inc.
303 San Mateo Boulevard NE
Albuquerque, New Mexico 87108-1382 USA
(888) 883-8203
www.americanabooks.com

ISBN: 1-58943-063-8

Library of Congress Cataloging-in-Publication Data

Henning, Dennis.
 Hiding under the table / by Dennis Henning with Patricia Woods.
   p. cm.
Summary: "Autobiographical account of a man suffering from an eating disorder and other addictions, and how he took responsibility for his own recovery" --Provided by publisher.
ISBN 1-58943-063-8 (pbk. : alk. paper) -- ISBN 1-58943-101-4 (audio cassette) -- ISBN 1-58943-102-2 (audio compact disk) -- ISBN 1-58943-103-0 (audio mp3 on compact disk) 1. Henning, Dennis--Mental health. 2. Compulsive eaters--United States--Biography. 3. Sex addicts--United States--Biography. I. Woods, Patricia. II. Title.

  RC552.C65.H466 2004
  362.196'8526'0092--dc22

                    2004022635

Contents

Preface

I wrote this book, not as guide for recovery, but as a tool that can help sufferers, family members, friends, and loved ones take a look at themselves and realize that they are not alone. You do not have to have experienced what I went through to learn from this book. If you can relate to my story at all, then you can see that there is hope.

My journey was not easy. It remains a constant reminder that each day I choose to *live*. My recovery is a process that evolves each day into more opportunities and choices, choices that define who I am now, not who I was in my past.

Take the time to feel whatever emotions the book brings you, knowing that the solutions you seek are out there. I am by no means telling you that my way is the only way, or that my way will work for you. My way worked for me, and I wanted to share that journey with you.

I want to say "thank you" with all my heart to the people who helped me start my journey and have stayed with me through the good, the bad, and lots of ugly in my life: My best friend and number one fan – my mom, Jeannette Henning, the one person I have admired my whole life. My brother, Richard, and his boys Andrew and Bo – who make my day no matter what. My first therapist, Preston Parsons; my grade school teacher, Mr. LaChappelle; my old roommate, Tod Feaster; Dr. William

Radar. Mr. Jeff Schwartz, who I learn from each day. My second family in Sacramento, the Slaughters. The gracious Cliff West. Mr. Mike Schwartz, who never stopped believing in me. Gay Harwin and Rod Lindblom, who have never given up on me. Blue Huber, whose passion for others rivals mine. Carol Mitchell, a mentor and diehard friend for life. Dr. Susan Ashley, who I am proud to call my friend. Dr. John Gardin, a friend and brilliant man who I am honored to know. Bob Timmons, for his knowledge and guidance. Gary Monroe, for championing my causes. Chuck Morris. Alyson Dutch, for believing in my story. George Lovato, CEO of Americana Publishing, who helped bring my dream to reality and gave me a chance to share my story when no one else would. Ted McClure for his understanding and brilliance and Pat Woods for helping to decipher my life and put it down on paper so others could share in my journey. I want to thank those people like me who have taken the time to share their stories so that others can see that hope and happiness are waiting around the corner. And I thank God.

Thank you,
Dennis Henning

Introduction

When I first met Dennis Henning in 1997, I had been in practice in the behavioral health field for over 20 years, specializing, as I still do, in substance abuse. Although I had treated scores of women with anorexia and/or bulimia, I had never met or treated a man who admitted to suffering from either condition. No wonder. Like so many of my colleagues at the time (and many of my colleagues today), I thought of eating disorders as primarily affecting women, and that any man so afflicted must be gay or must have been sexually abused, or both. So when Dennis shared part of his recovery story with me, and he was not gay and had not been sexually abused, he had my attention.

Dennis had a legitimate axe to grind. He found it next to impossible to get appropriate treatment for his eating disorder because he was a man. It is true that 10% or fewer of those *presenting* for treatment of an eating disorder are male, but that does not mean that men comprise only 10% of those *with* an eating disorder. In a field where it is still generally held that eating disorders affect women almost exclusively, and that if a man would happen to have an eating disorder he must be either gay or have a history of sexual abuse, why would any man who is not gay or who had not been sexually abused admit to having an eating disorder?

Yet for Dennis, his mission has never been solely about raising awareness about men with eating disorders or for advocating for treatment programs for men with eating disorders (although both are still great concerns). The issues for Dennis were, and are, broader than that – anyone, regardless of gender, should be able to get competent help for this devastating disease, and our views about this disease and whom it affects must change.

Our knowledge about eating disorders and about men with eating disorders is growing, in no small part due to the efforts of advocates like Dennis. We now know that men with eating disorders present with psychological, emotional, and mental issues similar to their female counterparts. Certainly there are gender-specific issues, as there are in any mental, emotional, and behavioral problem, but the similarities outweigh the differences. And the similarities exist not because men are somehow "feminized," but because eating disorders, whether affecting a man or a woman, are still eating disorders. We know that anorexia, bulimia, and binge eating affect 15% of the females in our country. We haven't a clue about how many men are affected. Dennis wants to change that, because in a field where 20% to 25% or more of those untreated die, we're talking about millions of lives at stake.

Dennis's crusade is not only for the effective and equitable treatment of eating disorders. He also has developed (and, in California, implemented) a model program for our public schools to educate our children about food and nutrition: THE NUTRITION & BODY IMAGE PROGRAM™. It is no secret that as a country we are in trouble. Approximately 60% of us are overweight and a third of those, or 20% of us, are obese. Eighty percent of our children are on a diet by the time they reach the fourth grade. More than 80% of our 10 year olds fear being fat. Our relationship to our bodies and to the food we eat is upside down and backwards, and it's not getting better.

Turn on the television, open a magazine, flip the pages of your paper, and you will read over and over again about the newest sure-fire diet. It's no wonder that Dennis's acronym DIET means Dangerous Identity Enhancing Trap, for about one-third of all dieters will become compulsive about their dieting. In other words, whether male or female, one-third of all dieters will graduate from dieting to an eating disorder. And Dennis wants to change that, too.

I can assure you that Dennis's story, in all its uncomfortable detail, is worth reading because it's a story of one man's triumph over not only his personal demons, but over a system that would have left him behind. And as if the journey were not enough, Dennis has shared with us the road map he developed and used to find his way out, an approach he calls *The Daily Process, 16 Points of Life*©. It's not the perfect map, and shouldn't be read as the only way past the grip of a debilitating mental disorder. But it is a map that you might just find will guide you or someone you love out of bondage.

In the pages of this book you will meet a man with whom you may not always agree, but who you will respect. You will meet a man who is outspoken in his views and unbridled in his passion for those at risk of developing an eating disorder, and for those already there. You will meet a man who has walked through his own hell, and can tell us about his journey back. And most importantly, you will meet a man of integrity, totally committed to changing the way you and I think about eating disorders, food, our bodies, and our lives.

I am proud to call Dennis my friend and privileged to introduce him to you.

> John G. Gardin II, Ph.D., Clinical Psychologist
> Adjunct Professor, University of New Mexico
> Albuquerque, New Mexico

For more information on *The Daily Process, 16 Points of Life*© and THE NUTRITION & BODY IMAGE PROGRAM™, see
http://www.nutritionbodyimage.com.

Hiding Under the Table

Chapter One: Four Episodes

Episode One

"I'm inviting everybody in class to my pizza party this Saturday for my birthday, except for Dennis Henning, because he'll eat *everything*," said Timmy. At that moment I could not move, I could not breathe and I didn't know what to do. Why, why would he do this to me in front of everyone? What did I do to him? I never said or did anything to him to deserve this.

I felt as though I had been kicked in the stomach and all the air had been knocked out of me. I sank into my chair hoping it would all go away. I just wanted to crawl out of my skin and become invisible. But I could not. I was seated in the front row in the middle of the classroom with nowhere to go.

Everywhere I looked, kids were laughing at me. I felt a scorching heat through my body and the sweat just pored over me as I sat there hoping it was a dream or just a joke. But it was neither. I could not look anywhere but at the top of my desk now, in fear that everyone was still looking at me and laughing. I laughed with them, hoping that they would stop laughing at me. I had no one to turn to at that moment for comfort or help. I was alone and felt like I was dying inside. I wanted to cry but knew it would only make things worse.

The kids kept laughing and the sound got louder and louder while I felt smaller and smaller. I was alone in the middle of over twenty kids. That sound of laughter directed at me was so painful and shaming, that to this day I get a burning feeling in my body and my palms get real sweaty and clammy when anyone asks me if I am going to eat all of my food at any one given meal, even if it is just a small meal. It's just like having a dream about being naked in front of other people; it's the sense of being exposed or helpless, without defenses or protection. To this day, I eat most of my meals alone because of this feeling of shame. It took years, but sometimes I am able to eat with people and *not* feel the shame I felt then.

The feeling I had that day in fourth grade has never gone away, no matter how hard I try to forget or let it go. My teacher did not stop them for what seemed like an eternity. I felt so much shame and guilt for not being invited and didn't know what I had done to this boy so he treated me this way. He said it with a smile on his face, knowing others would laugh and make fun of me.

As I sat there waiting for class to end, I was too scared to walk out because everyone would say more cruel things and tell other children what had taken place. I waited until everyone left before I got up to leave. As I stood up, I prayed with all my heart that no one would say anything; that they would just let it go. Of course, they didn't let it go.

As I headed to the door my legs felt as if they weighed a hundred pounds each. My fears came true when I walked out the door and all the kids laughed again. I was embarrassed, angry, and felt ashamed and guilty, but didn't know why. This kind of torture and cruelty was something I experienced every day while attending Catholic elementary and high schools in California. My brother and I frequently had to fight our way home from grade school. When our mother would ask how school was, I said it was okay – then asked her if we could go to McDonald's®. This was how I dealt with emotional pain.

I ate and ate and ate until I was numb, and that became my salvation. Food always made the pain go away. It was my friend who never made fun of me, never laughed at me, never made fun of my clothes, never judged me because we were poor and always made me smile. I had found something to cure my needs at such a young age that it became my solution to everything I could not face for the next 25 years.

"Oh please, Lord, let this stop … please help me … I can't handle this any more. I'll do whatever you want, just stop this," I begged and begged for what seemed like days, but in reality was just 24 hours. Why did God not help me? Why? I could not tell anyone around me that I was sick again because they would say, 'Here we go again, I thought you were better.' Well, so did I, but my way never worked. No one around me understood what I was going through and neither did I. It was not that they did not care. I did not share what I felt because I never really knew what I was experiencing or why.

I had caused enough pain in my family and did not want to cause more. Everyone who knew us always said I was the one who had the problems. Other people always said that I was why the family had problems. I hated being labeled like this, but it was true. I did cause problems, but I had no idea why. I could not explain what it was that made me eat and throw up all the time, abusing my body that way. I could not explain why I was so cruel to my mother, grandmother and great-grandmother. They only tried to love me. I hated myself so much that I hated everyone who tried to help me. If I accepted their love, then I would have to look at me and love me. I was not ready or even able.

It would be so easy for me to blame my family or society for all the things that went wrong in my life. My problems, pain, anger, self-hatred, and suffering were due to others. I could feel sorry for myself. I could make up stories about how I was abused as a child, say I was mistreated, never loved, and this is the root of my poor behavior. That would make me a victim and I could become someone that people could pity. But I cannot do that.

As an adult I find it ironic to see how I handled things as a child and the correlation between that and how I handled things as an adult. As a child I was constantly ridiculed. I felt shame and alienation from the other kids at school because of what my family did not have. I turned those feelings inward, while laughing it off in public. But I cried myself to sleep at night wondering what I had done wrong to those kids so they treated me poorly and tried to hurt my family and me.

My anger was so deep that all I wanted was for those kids to suffer and feel pain like mine. I didn't know how to retaliate against them. As an adult, I learned how to get even with them and so made up for all those years of suffering. The treatment I received became my excuse for my own behavior. Everything was someone else's fault. I blamed other people and situations for everything that went wrong in my life. My excuse was that people had always belittled my family because we were poor, on welfare, wore hand me down clothing, and my father was absent.

Food became my soothing friend and partner. It was the answer to everything until it became my identity. The kids I knew thought it was cool that I could out-eat them. Food would soothe my pain and make me feel zoned out. I ate burgers, fries, candy, cakes, sodas, fried food, and heavy foods with a high fat content. At ten years of age I knew these foods made me feel better and that they relieved the pain for that moment. The relief only lasted a short time, so I kept coming back for those feelings of security and love.

When I ate a lot of food in front of the some of the kids they seemed to idolize me. They made fun of me or laughed at me to my face, but they still seemed to like me. But the taunts and pain continued. My identity as a child and well into high school became wrapped up in food. Food took away my pain, became my friend in my loneliness. And I was alone most of the time.

I had no real friends to talk to, no-one who cared about me outside of my family – but I could not talk to them. All I had was food. The pattern was set early for how I related to others and life situations. Food was the answer to everything from my identity to friendship to coping.

I felt like a freak and had no idea if anyone else went through this. I felt guilty because I knew other people had worse lives than mine. But I couldn't stop eating. It was the only thing to numb my emotional pain. It kept me from killing the person I had become, a loser who could not control something as simple as food. I wasn't sure what I would do *physically* to myself or other people, while I was constantly attacking people *verbally*. I did know that if I physically hurt someone else I could go to jail, but if I hurt myself it was okay.

I ate so much that I could not breathe, thought I would explode, and felt so heavy and ugly. It felt as if my skin was crawling and going to crack at any minute. I was bruised all over from the massive amount of food I consumed.

My binge eating was out of control. A meal might consist of eight pieces of fried chicken, 10 peanut butter cups, six candy bars, an entire pizza, and five soft drinks. Each bite was a slow act of suicide for me. I knew I was not able to stop even though I wanted to.

My life was totally out of control on every level. Eventually my need for food would drive all the rest of my behavior. My binge and purge cycles meant I had to spend $300 or $400 a day on food. I didn't earn all that money by myself, so I found other ways to get the food or get the money, no matter who got hurt in the process. When I was older and sitting at my mother's house, I was afraid to leave or see anyone. I did not want them to see me eating, so I hid all the garbage and put it into the back of the car to throw it away later when no one was around.

Episode Two

"Please, God, please stop this," is all I could keep saying in a low whisper. Everything got very hazy for me at that time. I often felt as if I was on a cloud looking down at the destruction I had created. All I could think of was to find a way to stop the pain and agony. It seemed the only way to stop it from happening again was to die. However, I was so scared that I didn't think I could even do that right. How horrible can a life be when even suicide is too much to carry out? I didn't want to hurt someone else, but I felt as though I had no control over what I would do. I didn't want to live like this and I knew I had to find a way to help myself.

I told my mother we needed to call the police and have them put me in a hold in the county jail or psychiatric unit. I ended up in the county lockdown unit where I would not hurt myself or other people.

They only reason they did this was because our family had numerous friends in law enforcement. After speaking with an officer, my mother and I drove to the facility across from the University of California Davis Medical Center in Sacramento. I felt so embarrassed and scared. How did I get so bad that this was the only way to help me? Was I so weak that I couldn't help myself? The answer was clearly 'yes'. At that time I was living in such a distorted reality that I would have either killed myself or hurt someone else. In my mind it was all because of food.

The one thing I always turned to for help betrayed me again. Trying to cure myself with food just led me to more failure. As we sat in the car I told my mom I was okay, while knowing that I was getting worse. The sounds of cars and people passing by outside got louder and louder as we drove to the facility. I felt as though I was a big disappointment and failure to my family, which was the truth. I felt sad, hungry, angry, lonely, worthless, pathetic, and as if I would never get better. Was this what I had to do to keep my sanity? If so, I wanted to die as soon as possible because this felt like death to me.

We arrived at the facility and I just sat in the car. I didn't want to go in, but I knew it was the only way to help me at this time. I had no idea what would happen once I passed through the doors. I only knew that I had to stay 72 hours. The walk from the car to the inside seemed as though it took forever.

For me it was yet another day in which I could not control anything in my life due to the fact that food was all I could think about and all I wanted to make all the pain I felt go away. I cried as we entered the facility. I was in my early twenties at this time and had been struggling with my eating disorder for over six years. I didn't know if this stay would help me, but it would keep me alive for three more days. I hated myself for doing this, being so weak and unable to do this on my own. Being in a locked facility with people who were very mentally unstable was pathetic. But I realized once I was in there that I had deep emotional problems and was no different from the others who were there. We all just acted out in different ways.

I felt relief when the door closed behind me. I was not in charge at this time. I could not abuse myself with food because I would have no control over when or what I was to eat. It felt so good not to worry for those few moments.

As I checked in, they took my shoestrings and belt so I had nothing that could be used to hang myself or hurt anyone else. They put me in a room with two other men, one who thought he was Perry Mason, the television lawyer, and the other who thought he was Jesus Christ. The small beds had thin mattresses and hard pillows that were more like bricks. The bathrooms were shared by everyone and looked very unsanitary. The rooms smelled of dry sweat and lack of fresh air. Just going to the bathroom frightened me. I did not share why I was there. I lied because I didn't want someone to make fun of me. I thought this was a joke until the other two men quoted the bible and law in every argument. I was stuck with these people and it was sad and scary.

It was my choice to come here and yet I felt like a fool. Would I lose my mind like them or had I already lost it and just didn't know. While it was funny to hear the two men argue, I was too scared to even answer questions when they asked me. I stared at the walls and prayed to God for one more chance. One more chance and I would not lie, deceive, steal, manipulate, or hurt others or myself. I swore it up and down. Knowing that I could not and would not keep this promise, I just wanted out. I was very good at telling people what they wanted to hear, so I could have what I wanted without ever being responsible or accountable for what I said or did.

The second day my mom, my brother Richard, and his wife Carrie came to see me. I was excited and embarrassed. They brought me two quarts of chow mein. Just what I needed to soothe the pain I felt … FOOD! All I did was talk about the other mental patients and how I did not belong there. I lied, of course. That was exactly where I needed to be. When they left I wanted to go with them, but they could not take me. That night I cried because I realized for the first time the truth about myself. I had emotional problems to which I had no answers and, really, no one to help me. I felt alone. Why was I like this? What had I done to deserve this? Tomorrow I would get out and then all would be fine. At least that's what I kept telling myself to get through the night. I would make the necessary changes so I could exist in society and my family.

When my mom picked me up after my stay I realized I was not alone. I lied to mom and told her I was better and wanted to eat. I yelled at her to take me to eat, I didn't need to go home. I had one friend who was always there for me, waiting for me with open arms … food. We went straight to a restaurant where I ordered two double bacon cheeseburgers, onion rings, French fries, and a large coke. My best friend food was here and we were ready to rock and roll again. My pain was gone for the moment, until each bite had been chewed and I was down to my last French fry. When I ate that fry I felt as though I lost my best friend and wanted more, because without my best friend I was not able to cope with life as I knew it.

Episode Three

I was sitting in a restaurant in Venice, California, waiting to order my meal when the waitress approached. She mentioned the daily specials. I didn't want to hear them and let her know. I asked if they had chicken that evening and she said yes, but it wasn't prepared the way I like it so I asked about fish. I think chicken and fish were two meals cooks couldn't really screw up unless they didn't know what they were doing. So I ordered in a very calm manner swordfish with steamed veggies. I wanted the fish dry, with nothing on it, meaning no butter, oil, lemon, sauces, or seasoning. The vegetables needed to be crisp, not soft. I ordered an iced tea with no lemon. Simple, I thought. No problem (in my world).

I asked the waitress three times to repeat the order just so I knew she understood what I wanted and how I wanted it prepared. I could tell by her voice and the looks she gave me that she was unhappy when I asked her to repeat the order and that she thought I was little too crazed about my meal. That was fine with me; I had gone there to eat, not to make friends. I had a book with me and started to read and relax when the bus person came over with my tea. The tea had a lemon in it and no straw. I asked the bus person to call my waitress over and I explained again that I ordered tea with no lemon and I wanted a straw. I was upset now and really pissed off because I didn't think it should be so difficult to get a drink order right.

Soon I had my tea and read my book. The food runner came to the table with my meal. As she put it down, she asked if everything was okay. I noticed that it was not swordfish and the vegetables weren't steamed, they were in a cream sauce. I was livid, but kept somewhat calm. It was not the runner's fault since she had not taken my order and obviously the waitress had not checked it before it was brought out. The runner summoned the waitress to my table and I informed her of the wrong order. She did what so many servers do – she blamed the kitchen. I found this unacceptable. She took my order and then blamed the kitchen. We went over my order again and now 40 minutes had passed since I first ordered. The frustration and anger were building in me like a forest fire that was out of control. I was ready to pounce on anyone and everyone.

By the time an hour had passed I was really pissed off. I calmly asked the bus person to send the waitress to my table. I was going to cancel and eat elsewhere. As I spoke with the bus person, the waitress brought my meal. I was relieved and nervous at the same time. She placed the meal in front of me and it was the same damn thing as before!

The rage built to a climax. With all the strength I could muster I got up slowly, went to the kitchen, and yelled at the cook. "How could you not get the fish right, you stupid son of a bitch? This is the second time tonight. Do I have to do it myself? God damn it, does anyone know what they are doing here?" I was about to continue when I heard a voice behind me state in a very authoritative and threatening manner, "Step back from the kitchen." I turned around and it was a police officer and his partner standing there. The restaurant called the police because they were afraid I was going to hurt someone, and I may have because I was so angry. The police escorted me to the car and cuffed me before sitting me in the back seat.

I was scared and embarrassed, but they did not understand. I explained to them what had happened. I sat in the back seat screaming that the cook had fucked up my meal and that it was not right for me to be in this car. I told the officers I just wanted someone to fix the right meal and it shouldn't be that hard to do. After they calmed me down they said they did not want to arrest me on a foolish charge. I agreed, but I sat in the car for over two hours with them complaining about the meal and the service. I was going to jail over a meal. I realized how bad this looked after they let me go. It took me three months to get over this episode and unfortunately it did happen again years later. I would go to these ridiculous lengths over a meal. What was I capable of doing over something that really mattered? I was scared of myself from that point on. I isolated myself from people as much as I could over the next twenty years.

Episode Four

July 13, 1994, was a beautiful and peaceful day. I could see all the people below my window enjoying the sunshine and life. I was enjoying neither. I was in my apartment in San Francisco sitting in my big leather chair, rocking back and forth in a panic trying to find a rehabilitation center that could help me before I took my own life. It was so bad this day that nothing could help me and no matter who I called, hoping they would hear the pain in my voice, no one asked if I was okay. I wanted my mom or brother to ask me if I needed help, but I was so good at lying that they could not hear my desperation.

I called eleven rehabilitation centers for eating disorders all over the United States and Canada. Each had the same answer, we do not have a program for men, and since I had no money they would not even discuss admissions with me.

I could not believe what I heard. All these places only helped women and some even said that men do not suffer from eating disorders. The money situation made me more depressed and I had no health insurance.

As I sat there the pain in my legs and arms became more intense. The burning and stinging was like a hot prod on my flesh. Blood was everywhere. I used a razor and fork to help me get through the emotional distress of each rejection. I used the razor to slowly slice my legs and arms and then sat there with relief that I still cannot describe. To stop the constant rocking back and forth, I used the fork to stab my legs and arms. I always made sure the cuts were not deep enough so others could ask about them. I did not want scars. This time I went too far. I wanted relief at that moment and I got it.

This episode lasted for over six hours and it took almost a year for the marks to disappear. I did not realize the damage I had done to myself. I knew where physical pain came from. But I still didn't know what started the emotional pain, so I had no idea what was happening and how to stop it. I knew the cutting would stop it, or at least I thought so at the time. My anger was so strong because of my inability to help myself that I started punching myself all over my body and then I threw myself against the wall at a full run. This almost knocked me out, but it brought relief. Hitting doors and walls, throwing myself against them. I thought the physical pain would make me forget the pain in my head.

When I hurt myself physically it numbed the emotional hell I lived in. I finally spoke with a wonderful woman at a facility in Los Angeles. We worked out a deal with my family's help. I would enter the facility on July 14, 1994. I thought it was funny that I was going into a rehab center for an eating disorder and the person who picked me up at the airport allowed me to go to Burger King and eat a double whopper, onion rings and a soda. What was even funnier is that I bought her dinner as well.

Chapter Two: Childhood

Like so many other people, my childhood was painful and difficult for many different reasons. Some reasons I understood, because children do and say things not knowing why they do so, or what the words they say really mean. Sometimes I had no idea why children were so cruel. Why would the children make fun of my mom and grandma? They had worked hard their entire lives to make my life the best it could be. What had they ever done to deserve this? Why did kids laugh at my clothes or what my mom and grandma wore?

I realized much later in life, after working on the anger and hate I felt for all those kids in school, that children's main view of life is what they see from their parents. Many parents want to blame society for their children's dysfunctional behaviors and lifestyles because it is easier not to be responsible and accountable for their children. Most children act like their parents, taking on their prejudices, ignorance, biased opinions, and cruel behaviors. This occurs because children will mirror what they see and hear. Children are told how to behave, what to say, and, if they disobey their parents, they are punished. In order for them to avoid pain and punishment, they do as they are told.

The coping skills I learned as a child to protect myself carried over into adulthood for me. Food always made each encounter I faced better. The anxiety I felt each day disappeared when I ate. The food soothed all the emotional pain, while the physical pain only lasted for a moment. As I grew older, I learned that I must deal with my past by seeking help to find answers. I also learned that I could not solve my problems alone, no matter how hard I tried.

While I was in grade school, I was one of three children who seemed to be singled out each day for abuse and taunts by my classmates and even some teachers. I wanted to transfer to a public school, but it would not have been beneficial for me in terms of my education. My family simply did not understand why I wanted to transfer, because I never told them the truth about school. Many nights I cried myself to sleep or would eat late night meals in order to calm myself down. I feared going to school every day, but could never tell my mother because she worked so hard and sacrificed so much to put us in private school.

Many of the conflicts I faced in school originated because my mother, grandmother, and great-grandmother were rearing my brother Richard and me. For some reason, the children made fun of this and the fact that we had no father. To this day I will defend my family on any slight I perceive made toward them. Now I do it with calm and maturity; back then it was with words and fists.

Although we attended a Catholic school, the teachers did nothing to stop the torment from the other children. While they threatened to punish the children who made remarks, wrote on my desk, stuck tacks under my seat as I was sitting down and laughed at me when I could not spell, they never really did punish the children. The abuse just continued.

When I reached seventh grade, I finally found an ally, someone I could talk to about my problems. My teacher took me under his wing and taught me that I did not have to fight back because the students made fun of me. He tried to teach me to let it go. It was hard to listen to him because by that time I had suffered through six years of torment with no relief. He would take several of his students to a hot dog joint for lunch and it was great to have the attention and time from another adult who cared about us. Since I had no father figure, this attention was very special to me. He didn't play favorites and corrected us all when we were wrong. He even helped me later in life, when I ran up my mom's telephone bill and had no money to pay. Without his help my mother would have lost her telephone service because of my irresponsibility.

Although I now understand why children act cruelly toward others, there are times when the pain from the past is still very real to me. I don't turn to food to soothe myself today; I turn to the people who I have come to trust and love, and to my own instincts. I examine my feelings to determine what is really bothering me. Today, I have the knowledge that I have choices that I didn't know about before, or was afraid to make because then I would have to be responsible. Now, with each choice I accept the outcome so I can learn and grow as a person.

During lunch at school I would have two sandwiches and a blueberry pie, eat every bite, and then go back for more if there was time. My mother and grandmother worked in the school cafeteria to help pay tuition and receive some help for school lunch money. The other children would always say we were the welfare family and living on charity. My mother and grandmother worked for everything we got and nothing was ever given to us. My family accepted no charity, but the jibes still hurt.

When I came home from school my great-grandmother would gently rub my arms, back and neck with her hands.

It was a very peaceful feeling, and I felt loved and cared about. I would daydream while she did this because it was fun and brought me happiness. It taught me that I could go places in my mind where no one could hurt me, so it became my own paradise.

As an adult, despite my sex addiction, I didn't like to have people touch my body. My sex addiction was about my need for affection and control over other people. The fear and anxiety I experienced when they touched the disgusting body I had in my mind was too much for me to handle. Even when my body fat dropped to the single digits, I felt fat, ugly, disgusting, and ashamed. My mental body image was distorted. I could only see myself through a perception of fat. These distorted views prevented me from experiencing any real intimacy with the women I knew. I missed out on so much of life from my lack of intimacy.

I was a large child, not heavy, but large in that I was big for my age. At a young age I learned that the more I ate the bigger I would be, and thought I could defend my family and myself if I got bigger. I was taught that the bigger men are manlier. Although the truth is that being a man has nothing to do with your muscles, weight, or height, I believed what I was taught. Being a real man is about being responsible for your actions, aware of who you are and are not, and not what others want you to be to fit their own needs. Women face certain societal issues about what is necessary to be accepted and I faced those same issues from my childhood through adulthood. I just never learned to be a macho man – nor did I want to be one.

As a child I always dreamed of helping other people who suffered the same abuse I did. I wanted to help them overcome pain, anger, and frustration. Witnessing their pain made me sick to my stomach. I always stood up for other people as much as possible, even though it sometimes turned physically violent when I got into a fight. My life now revolves around helping others like me to overcome whatever challenges they face from the past in order to build a healthier lifestyle and learn to love themselves.

Because my mother, grandma, and granny loved us so much, the kids always called me "momma's boy" and other harsh, cruel names. They laughed at my last name and called me chicken, hen, fag, sissy, queer, and made comments because I had no dad. The kids would say he left because of me, and they knew he was an alcoholic and called him names as well. I built up a hate for him for abandoning my mom, my brother, and me. Later in life I learned to forgive what he did. He was a sick man and did not really know what he had done or was doing while drinking.

My parents had been married for five years when I was born. My brother Rich was born a year and two weeks before me. My father made life a living hell for my mom with his drinking and abuse. Having two children to care for gave my mother courage to leave my father. She filed for divorce when I was six months old because he came home one night and tried to beat her and get at my brother and me. My mother put herself in harm's way without hesitation to protect us and keep him away. Because my mom's lawyer did not file the correct papers she was never divorced. The years passed and there was no divorce.

My mother tried to make me feel better by saying the other kids had a hard life and their cruelty was just their way of venting their own frustration. They tried to hurt someone else because they had been hurt. It was not what I wanted to hear. I didn't like being their target. But, for whatever reason, I was. Later on in life I did to others as the kids did to me. I understand the reasons why I hurt others. I did it to hide from pain and felt that if I could hurt them then I would feel better about my own issues and not having to heal with my pain as much. My reasoning was faulty and unacceptable. I know that now. I have no excuses for the pain and suffering I have caused family, friends, and complete strangers.

When I see children playing sports with their fathers, I always wonder about them. Since I did not have a dad around, I have never known what I have missed. I can only guess what my life may have been like if I had a dad to discipline me and teach me things. Mom did it all and better than most two-parent homes. Because of my dad's behavior, I have had abandonment issues deeply rooted in my soul. I have faced them all my life.

Being poor and fatherless were two big reasons why the kids always shamed me. It was even worse when they also made fun of me for having my mom and grandma at the school working to help pay tuition and for food. These kids did not stop. I took the anger I felt from this abuse out on mom and grandma, and didn't want them to be around or to be seen with them. I thought that would make it better; all it did was hurt them unnecessarily. My anger hurt those I loved, then and even later in life.

I thought if I could stop them from coming to school, picking me up, and always being there each day, it would stop the kids. It never did. The pain I felt in my stomach every day, knowing that I would be laughed at and ridiculed because of my clothes, difficulty in class or family, just killed me. My rage grew and I directed it toward the only people who really cared, my mom and grandma. I never wanted this to happen to anyone I loved or cared about.

Sadly, when I got older I continued to hurt all those who loved me and care about me over and over and over again. Why? I was a coward. I could never face up to so many things because it was better to blame my family for what went wrong, rather than make what I wanted to happen become a reality through being honest about myself and what I could and could not do.

Food was my higher power because I believed it would take all the hurt away and I did not have to do anything. Twenty years later I realized food was not the answer to my problems. It took 30 years to learn that I had options and choices other than food in order to heal my mind, body, soul, and spirit. As I grew older, I swore that, once I graduated from high school, no one would ever break me or keep me down. Little did I know I was to become my own worst enemy before I learned that food was not the answer.

Growing up in a house with three women had advantages and disadvantages. My great-grandmother and grandmother always tried to tell my mother what she was doing wrong rather than applauding her for rearing us the way she did. The arguments they had while we were growing up and into adulthood frightened me. These arguments made me sick, emotionally and physically. Sometimes I cried at night or in the back yard because I was afraid they would leave after every fight. I would soothe the pain by sneaking into the kitchen at night and eating something. It was always better after I ate.

During an argument, I would jump in and try to calm the situation, but it didn't help. I only made things worse. As I grew older, I became so overbearing in arguments that no one had a chance to respond. I scared or shamed them into behaving differently from the way they did when I was a child. I did this out of my fear of being abandoned. As I watched my family in these situations, I learned that I had to yell or dominate to be heard and get what I wanted.

This behavior continued for more than 20 years, when my mother and grandmother lived together. The constant yelling, threats, and verbal abuse they used on each other was harsh. Later on I talked to them about it and learned this was how they grew up, facing mental and physical abuse from family and husbands. They reacted the only way they knew how. The cycle of abuse was well established in our family.

My mother and grandmother loved each other so much, but they didn't know how to communicate with each other or be responsible for their actions. Each blamed the other for the arguments and then, later on, acted as though nothing had happened. But I saw the pain on their faces, and it killed me because I couldn't do anything about it. Each one had a reason for her beliefs and actions. They lived together this way until my grandmother's death. My mother still hasn't gotten over the pain of losing her best friend. And I fear that day when my best friend, my mom, is no longer here with me.

Both of these women were strong and courageous about their lives. They never gave up and always looked for solutions rather than just problems. My mom's father was a brute of a man who never had anything to do with our family while we were young. My grandfather was an abusive alcoholic who beat my grandma and anyone who got in his way. He would beat them so badly that, when my mother was three, she and my grandma left home and hid out from him and his family for nine years, out of fear they would be killed. I hated this son of a bitch all my life, even though I didn't meet him until later in life.

He had six brothers and sisters and only one was not an alcoholic. He and his brothers would go into a bar and knock off the hats of all the gentlemen, then dare anyone to pick them up. When the men or women attempted to retrieve their hats, my grandfather and his demented brothers beat them mercilessly. I used to think I would be like them some day because of my anger and hate for those who hurt my family and me. I was like them in a way because I would abuse myself physically as well as emotionally. It seemed so hard as a young man to find any type of role model because my father and other male relatives were men who abused alcohol and cared for no one but themselves.

When I was a child my mother would tell me about my dad and his abuse. The worst thing I remember is how she would compare me to him and my grandfather, making me hate myself even more. But she said it was the only way she could defend herself when we fought. To me, any man who would do what my father and grandfather did was less than human and he did not deserve to live.

For years I thought I would be like them, and I fought against it every day. As a child you believe what parents say if it is pounded into you enough. I not only hated them, but hated myself for what I thought I would become and, with the grace of God, have never been. But words leave scars that take years to heal.

I met my father on two occasions. Each time he gave money to my brother and me, but nothing else. He had no answers as to why he left and did not come back. No reasons for not finding us or being there for us. Not one dime to help my mom and us all those years. Nothing. In 1985 I had been speaking with my father once a month while I was living in New York. He had cirrhosis of the liver from alcohol abuse. We spoke on a Monday and he agreed to meet me to talk about the past. By this time I understood a little about his addiction and being sick. Mom helped by telling me he was my father and I needed to seek some type of relationship with him.

We arranged to meet on Saturday in San Francisco. I flew to California on Saturday morning and discovered he had been hospitalized but on Friday night had discharged himself, bought some beer, and drank himself to death in a sleazy hotel. After all these years he still could not overcome his addiction to meet me. I felt numb when I heard this and didn't know what to do or who to call. I did what I always did, which was to turn to food. That day I spent over $400 on food to numb the pain and embarrassment. I had failed again in another relationship. It was a pattern to follow in my life. When anything bad happened I ate and ate and ate and ate.

At times I still miss what I never had with my father, and I will always feel that void. But I no longer turn to past behaviors and actions to deal with the pain. I choose to talk and figure out what and why I feel what I feel at that moment. I am no different from other people, but I have found help and focus to make the right decisions for me, not decisions based upon what other people think.

My lack of growth as a person was easy to blame on others because I did not have to try. I liked having my family and other people feel sorry for me, fearing what I would do if they did not do as I asked or demanded. I was that big ugly bully I always hated when growing up. I became that person I hated in all those kids who hurt and tortured me. But food always made everything better.

My eighth grade year at Holy Cross Grade School in Bryte, California, did not go fast enough for me. I counted down the days from the beginning of school to my graduation. I looked forward to starting high school and getting away from all the abuse and having the opportunity to start over with new kids and teachers. I knew some of the kids from my class were also going to Christian Brothers High School, but I thought I could avoid them with so many new classmates to meet. It was a dream to go and be accepted and be myself without the laughing and ridicule I had faced for the past eight years.

The summer between grade school and high school was filled with sports and family. I felt like a big shot going to Christian Brothers High School in Sacramento. It was my time to shine. It turned out to be nothing I had expected or wanted. I thought grade school was the worst time in my life. High school made grade school seem like Sunday school. But, I still had my best friend with me as always to take away the pain and suffering I would go through each day. For some reason I was a simple target for kids to ridicule and shame. The torture continued in high school. I thought that since my mother and grandmother did not work at the school it would help with the abuse, but it was no different.

A positive aspect of school was that I could really choose who I spent time with and trusted. It seemed as if I became friends with people who had also suffered as I did without provoking the treatment we faced. The school was an all boys school and I was excited to be there. The school had so much history and pride and I wanted to be a part of that. My brother was a star baseball and basketball player his freshman year so I thought I could fit in as well. But, I never really did. In high school I ate more than I ever thought I could. It made me feel better during school as well as at home when I had to deal with family issues and the anxiety of going to school the next day. Not having a father was very difficult for Richard and me because there were so many father-son activities we could not attend. We felt sad and ashamed because of it. The other kids laughed at us for not having a father. My brother was a top student and athlete for all four years he was at the school. Nothing was ever given to him; he worked for all of it. But we still felt the shame.

I had to struggle, but I made all the sport teams and was known for my rough play and intensity. Even though I played, I always took grief from the other players because I wanted to play on the first team and thought I should – so I never gave up. One good thing I have always had is the belief that I could do what I set my mind to and this was good. But it also drew harsh criticism from many kids and coaches.

During my junior year our basketball team went to the state finals and I played very little, but I was on the team. I had 32-inch thighs and a 36-inch waist. I was big and they called me blockhead because I looked like a square. I hated that name and the constant laughing at me because I was so large. I knew the food soothed all my pain and allowed me to accept the pain. I just thought that this was how life would be.

My large appetite became my identity. The other kids talked about it but never shamed me for it. They knew I would share my lunch if they were hungry or did not have lunch. During my brother's freshman year in high school, his basketball team went to a tournament in Woodland, California. After a game, we stopped by McDonald's® to eat. I ate twelve Big Macs and the guys were really impressed. It felt good to have them talk with me. I could even out-eat Steve Bruce, their big eater.

Another time we went to buy ribs with some of the guys, and Steven and I had a standoff over the last rib. I went for it and he stabbed me in my right hand with his fork. It hurt but it was more fun than anything. I liked to be accepted and not shamed and ridiculed.

I had daily fantasies of being a hero and saving the world or people in some way, thinking that people would stop hurting me. I carried these fantasies into adulthood, knowing that the pleasure of helping others far outweighed the pain I dealt with on a daily basis. I created characters in my head who were bad people who wanted to hurt others and I put myself in harm's way to prove I am a good person. I thought all the people who had hurt me would see this side of Dennis Henning.

Dating was something I couldn't even consider until my junior year. I wore really thick glasses and with my short hair I looked real dorky. I did not really know anything about girls or how to approach them or even how to ask them to dance. It was awkward because I did not have anyone to talk to about girls and relationships. Mom never brought it up and the only thing I knew about women came from an experience I had in fourth grade.

I had a classmate named Richard who sat in the back of the class with me. He kept looking at a book while the teacher had her back turned. I wondered what it was and he finally showed me this book called Men. Later on I learned it was a porn magazine. I had never seen a naked woman before and certainly never imagined women doing what the women in the magazine were doing. This was the beginning of my sexual education and not the way anyone should learn about sex. I became obsessed with these magazines and would always look at them in stores, which would get me in trouble with my mother and the store clerks.

While living in Bryte, we had neighbors who had a daughter my age. We used to hide behind the garage next to her house and show each other our body parts without touching. The excitement we felt while waiting to do this each day continued to build. To us it was innocent. One day her father caught us and it made what we did seem dirty and disgusting. That was his opinion of it. No one ever explained love and sex to me as a young man. This is where my sex addiction started to grow. My addiction to sexual adventures didn't fully blossom until I was twenty.

While in high school I dated one woman who was just the best. We were from completely different backgrounds and still we had something that brought us together. Her family was wealthy; mine was poor. She was a great student and I was not, but somehow we clicked together for a time. Katie was the first girl I ever kissed and the first of my sexual encounters. I remember walking almost a mile during the summer to her house. I would sneak upstairs and we would fool around while her parents were downstairs. The excitement of the sexual pleasure and the thought of getting caught made it all worthwhile.

I lost my virginity with Katie, but the relationship ended after my senior year. While kids always talked about their sexual escapades I never discussed mine nor have I ever since then because those relationships are between my partner and me.

While my school years laid the groundwork for the anger and rage I had for many years, I now realize that I helped create many of my own problems in life once I was on my own. I used every excuse in my head to avoid repeating my school experiences. I swore I would never let anyone hurt me, shame or degrade me for what I said, did, dressed, or anything else about my family or me.

This rage, combined with the self-hate I felt because I thought I was nothing, just like the kids said, pushed me further into my love affair with food and compulsive behaviors. I learned to medicate myself with food, sex, gambling, self-mutilation and physical abuse, degrading games, and a dangerous lifestyle. I wanted someone else to take my life because I was too cowardly to do it myself for fear of screwing it up. It was me against everyone else and no one was going to take away my best friend and confidant. I went through school depressed, angry, hurt, shamed, ridiculed and sad, without anyone to turn to for help.

It is sad when I look back and see that as a child when I went to school I had a snack from home, lunch money, and then my mom and grandma would bring me a McDonald's®, Taco Bell®, or other fast food at lunch. I ate and ate whenever I could at school to get the peaceful serenity food gave me so I did not have to deal with the pain I endured daily.

Mom never questioned my want and need for food and the large quantities I would eat. My mom's generation thought it was manly to eat large quantities. Her generation didn't realize someone could use food to deal with emotional pain. I was a boy and it was okay to eat that way. I was even encouraged to eat big portions and then ask for more. No one in my family had ever heard of an eating disorder when I was growing up. Somehow, and for some reason, I learned early the value of food as the anesthetic for all my struggles. Since I had no other outlet to help me, I found the comfort in food I lacked from other people. Since we had such a hard time financially, I did not want to put more of a burden on mom since I was a big burden as it was.

Food was a very important part of our immediate family and extended family life. My grandma cooked what seemed like day and night every day of my life. She cooked large meals for us, or family friends who came to visit. We always had something to eat if company arrived. We learned not to waste food because we were poor and other people were starving. I ate more than my share when I was little. I remember my grandmother and aunts always asking me if I was hungry when I would see them. If I said I was not hungry, they would say I didn't like their food, or I didn't love them. Even though they meant it as a passing statement, it hurt me. I loved them very much and did not want to hurt their feelings or have them think I did not love them. So I ate and ate and ate. I equated food with love and as an adult my relationships were with women who were great cooks.

During holiday dinners our extended family would get together. We would have 30 to 60 people under the same roof. It was chaos, but fun as well. All the kids ate in a separate room where we had fun. It was nice not having the adults tell us to eat this or that. I had no problems being told to eat. I just ate. The food was abundant and we could eat all we wanted. Even when we were full the adults would tell us to eat so we would stay out of their way.

Food meant love to me. If the adults did not want us around, the food made the unpleasant feelings go away. As a child I was always told that I needed to eat to be bigger and stronger. Big and strong for what? I did not know. But I ate as I was told because I thought that the adults knew what they were talking about. Now, of course, I realize after all these years of food addiction that eating large portions does not make you big and strong. Eating for attention is harmful mentally and physically. Food helps the body and mind grow, but it also becomes a nurturing stimulus to turn to when depressed. Food is like an illegal or legal drug in the world.

Mom never let Richard or me go without, no matter how hard she and grandma had to work to provide us with everything we needed. Grandma worked for the families of the kids who went to my school. These were the same kids who tortured me. She worked as a caretaker for their grandparents. She would clean their homes, make their meals, and clean up after the kids and the families. She did this not because it was her job, but because it was the type of person she was, someone who cared. She was a hard worker who never complained, then she would come home and do it all over again for our house.

My grandmother was Winifred Armstrong and she was the rock of Gibraltar. She was never sick until three days prior to her death. She was the bravest woman I know. She never let her fears or her dysfunctional life stop her from trying each day to better herself and those around her. My grandma died in February, 1994, before I made my last attempt to deal with my eating disorder and other issues that controlled my life. She would always go with me to see my therapist in Oakland. We would stop and have a hamburger and fries on the way home.

For years I hated myself because I always wanted to go alone and would lie to her, telling her I wasn't going. She loved to go out for rides and something inside me made me lie to her for no reason. She never hurt me. All she did was love me and I would go out of my way to be cruel and hurt her. I did this for no other reason than that I wanted to control everything she and mom did, because I was a coward. I can never tell her again what I have been able to accomplish in life. But I know she sees everything and is proud of me. She was always a lady. No matter who hurt her, she always forgave them – especially me.

Saying I'm sorry can never make up for what I did and that is something I must live with each day of my life. I was living in San Francisco in 1994. My eating disorder was so out of control I had no idea what to do. No matter how much effort I put in to getting better, it didn't work. I decided to end everything because I didn't want to go on as I had been. I made a vow to myself that although it was selfish and cowardly, I would end everything if I could not make it one week without binging and purging and abusing myself. I made my list of things to do and I knew it would not be accomplished. Therefore, I had to end my life. The pain in my head would not go away. There was only one way to rid myself of this nightmare I called my life.

I made every excuse not to go home to see my grandmother who was dying from leukemia. I didn't want to leave my apartment and let anyone see me. I was paranoid as hell. Mom explained how bad the situation was and I finally agreed to go. I had to take a bus because mom could not come get me. She needed to be with grandma, but I thought that was just selfish and wrong of her. What about me? I was so angry that I had to take a bus that I was angry with grandma for being sick. She did nothing to be sick, it's just what it was, and I was a complete asshole.

I was so sick that the only person who meant anything to me was me. I couldn't see past that at the time, nor did I want to. I sat on the floor the night grandma passed away, just one day past her 76th birthday. I was so scared and nervous and I didn't want to be there. I was not able to help her or console my mom at a time she needed me. I was home for three days and she passed away in the hospital bed in the emergency room with my brother, mother and me in the room. I watched as her last breath left her body and it was something I will never forget. I screamed and slid down the wall, wanting that moment to be just a dream, knowing that the one person who loved me unconditionally was gone.

I could not handle this and it became another excuse for me to stay sick and have others feel sorry for me. My grandma died and I loved the fact that other people were worried about what I might do to myself. I didn't want to come home in the first place, because I thought she would be fine. This was another typical example of my denial of reality and not caring about the needs of others. I used her death to stay focused on myself and no one else. I then decided that I was going to get better for her, although I never followed through. I could never follow through on any one day; let alone change my life because my grandma died. This was so typical of me as well. I would say I would change because of something happening in my life. It gave me hope, but it was false hope.

I ate so much at the house the day people came over to pay their respects that I could barely walk. I hated myself for years because I was not able to be there when my mom needed me the most. I was not there for my mom as I could have been. I was able to forgive myself once I realized that what I had done was a reaction to my fears and disease. It was not the person I have struggled and fought to become today. It is difficult to allow myself to be okay with my past, but it is the one thing that allows me to grow each day. Forgiveness is the key. Once I learned to forgive myself, I learned to forgive others. It is a part of the foundation I build each day in order to live the life I can be proud of and deserve. My grandma is an angel now, and she makes a difference in my life every day. Her work ethics and integrity were never matched by anyone I have ever met in my life.

My mom and grandma were never apart once my brother and I were born. They lived together, with my great-grandma Adeline Waterston nearby and then living with them as she grew older. These three women battled abuse and dysfunctional relationships all their lives. They never gave up hope that one day things would be better. It is a hope I carry with me each day, as one of life's lessons that they taught me. Unfortunately these ladies never had outlets to seek help for themselves. Since they had to survive anyway they could manage, they did not think twice about the outcome of their screaming and arguing with each other. I learned this behavior and how to scream and yell from them. It was how they solved issues and whoever yelled the loudest or had the last word won. I was always scared they would go through with their threats to leave. I always made things worse by yelling even louder and never backing down. Communication was not something I learned until many years later!

These three ladies sacrificed their own personal and social lives so my brother and I would have the best of everything they could give us. We never went without because these women would not let us go without. My mom and grandmother would sleep on the floor and couch when we were younger, and even when I was in high school, so we had a bed. Whatever we wanted they would get, no matter how hard they had to work to do it, in order to satisfy our needs. My mom was a bus driver, janitor, housekeeper, nurse, a teacher's aide, and she would do every little job she could to provide for us.

As I got older and needed money, I would never take a job that was legitimate and could provide for me. I was too ashamed to just do something as mom and grandma had done. There was nothing to be ashamed about other than I was not the son, brother, or grandson anyone would want to claim at that time.

I do not blame my family or anyone else for what I have been through as an adult. Yes, I wish the kids had been different, but I know kids get their ideas, actions, and behaviors from their parents at times. For some reason I was a bad seed for many years. I lived this way to survive and like a scavenger I fed off others for my own dysfunctional life. I have never given up on my dreams and they are now coming true. What I have learned is that I did not know at the time of my actions what I was doing to others would cause trauma and damage beyond repair. I know I have done and said many things to destroy others because I wanted to never feel the pain I felt as a child.

Today I feel that pain at times and it is okay. I understand now why things happened. Whether or not I like it, it's what it is. I make choices not to react or respond as I did in the past because I know the consequences are too great. I am just a man, not superman, or Christ, or better than anyone. I believe we all have a purpose here and it takes time to find that and more pain than we ever want to know. My pain is no different than anyone else's. If I can change, then it is possible for anyone to change for the better. I listen now, hear what it is I am doing before I do it, and I see the consequences before I react. This is uncommon for me because I never had any simple every day tools for living.

My best friend, cheerleader in life, and the most unconditionally loving person I have ever known is my mom, Jeannette Henning. I learned from my mom that the finer things in life are how you treat those around you and what you do on a daily basis to better your own life no matter what someone else does or says – how you sacrifice what you have for the betterment of others, because it all comes back to us in ways we never expect. The finer things are not our cars, clothes, homes, vacations, money, or possessions.

My mom and grandma came from simple backgrounds and lived non-materialistic lives. They taught us that material things do not make you a better person. Their love and caring made them the great ladies they have been in my life, to me and to others. The material things, at the end of the day, will not make us better people. It took me years to realize that. It is the people we love and who love us that make our lives great. No possession in the world is going to love you as your family can love you. My mom taught me all these years to love others because that is how she lives her life. No matter what someone did or said, she always forgave them. When I was young I looked at this as being weak, but she is the strongest person I have ever been blessed to know.

Growing up, I was dyslexic in grade school and high school. I had no idea, until I went to college, that I had this problem. My biggest fear was reading out loud in school or discussing what we just read. Kids slammed me as stupid and slow, but my mom told me it was okay, that some kids start slow but become leaders in this world. I thought she did it to make me feel better and it did. This is just one way she helped me through rough times. No matter how much help and love she gave me, food was still what healed my pain. I felt so cool eating all that food, not knowing it was setting me up for the eating disorder that would eventually almost take my life. I thought this was normal even when I was full. I cried as a young boy if I could not have the food I wanted, and when I got older I cried because the food that I wanted was killing me and I had no way to stop. I did not know I had a problem with food until I was in my twenties.

I didn't know until years later why I was like this and that I could change my view of me and the world around me. Mom did not have a great life growing up, but she had what my grandmother could give her, as my brother and I had what our mom could give us. As we were not a family that talked about anything emotional, I did not know until I was an adult that the abuse and suffering in my mom's life was behind what she said and did. She did what most hurt and wounded people do – strike out at others in the only way they know how. When people are hurt they do to others what was done to them. I became an expert at doing this in my own life. If I was to suffer, then others would, too.

My relationship with my mom has been the one that I could always count on no matter how we treated each other or what we said. My mom and grandma are the only ones in my life that have really never told me to give up my dreams. That bond with my mom and grandma was very strong then and is equally strong now. Throughout my life and to this day, many people I encounter, either friends or foes, always tell me I should try something different in life because what I have tried at times has taken a long time to become reality.

I see these people as those who are not willing to take chances because of fear of failure and that they cannot make changes they would like to make, so they try to stop those around them from changing. I have learned that many dysfunctional people will try to stop others from advancing in life because they are afraid to try. That is fine, but they should not try to destroy others because they themselves will not take chances. It's funny how these people in my life always jumped on board when things went well, and would not accept their own responsibility if things failed.

Chapter Three: Body Image

I remember seeing the movie *Mask* with Eric Stoltz and Cher. It is an amazing story about a young man named Rocky who was viewed by other people as being physically disfigured. Those who knew him thought he was perfect. I cried throughout the movie. I viewed myself as disfigured and thought no one wanted to be around me because I looked so repulsive. Rocky was not repulsive, he had a beauty that shined brighter than the stars. During one scene in the movie he went to a carnival that had the mirrors that change the way you look on the outside. The mirrors make people look taller, thinner, heavier, shorter, bigger muscles, thinner thighs, perfect cheek bones. These mirrors played on the emotions of those who would dream of being different. We believe if we look better then everything else in life would be better.

I didn't need a mirror to tell me or show me that I was ugly, overweight, huge, and basically hideous. I had felt this way since I was a child and never thought any different about myself or my body until I was in my late 30s. This is how I felt about my body and my inability to make it better, so it was true to me. No matter what compliments I received I hated myself more because I believed these people were lying to me and I did not want to be around them if they could not tell me the truth about my body. I knew how I looked, things these people could not see.

While growing up I was always proud that people made comments about the amount of food I ate and my size. Since I did not have friends and was not good in sports, this felt good – to be accepted for something. I felt that even though the kids and adults were laughing at my eating habits, at least they noticed me. I felt shame for eating so much but it felt good emotionally. I was a large child and proud. One year I had the biggest size pants in Little League and still they were too small. But it brought me attention. After each game we got a hot dog and soda. I tried to be first in line and then I'd wait around to see if there was another hot dog for me. Since I was not that good and had to really work at sports, food was the only reward for all the shame I felt each game. During this time I came to realize that if I were bigger than other kids they would back down from me if I ever had to fight. So, I thought that being bigger helped. They still made fun of me.

Growing up in a household with three women who always thought eating was healthy made life difficult. We had no idea the food we ate could be unhealthy for us or that one day it would be my cure for everything. My family thought if you did not eat you were sick. I didn't want to disappoint them. As a child I did not know that my eating so much was odd or abnormal. This was how I ate and the family around me ate. I knew no different. In high school I started to see the difference in myself and others and how bodies developed differently.

Some people are lean, muscular, heavy, stocky, thin, or very large. I did not realize the pressures that went along with how my body would be and what others would say about my food intake and build. I saw how girls judged us in the same way we judged them. Since I was not attractive or built well I never cared about my weight.

Since the emotional pain did not change once I went to high school, neither did my eating habits. My food was my salvation for all four years. In high school food became my identity even more. The more I ate the more people noticed me. As in grade school, I had no friends that I could really talk to or share anything with, so it was really lonely.

During my junior year I started to really think about my body because kids would call me blockhead or block because of my size. They said I looked like one big block. To some people this would be a compliment. To me it was degrading and shameful. I felt pathetic that I was noticed this way, but it was the only way I had any attention other than never backing down for what I believed in. Also, I had my first relationship that year. I was always scared that the girls would laugh at me like the guys did. So I didn't spend much time trying to meet any or be around them. Even though I never heard any negative comments from girls I felt anxiety being around them and the fear that they would laugh at me as well. I avoided being around others as much as possible. These fears led to my need to isolate myself later in life from everyone who knew me.

I started dating Katie my junior year. She was beautiful and went to St. Francis, an all girls' school across town. I was amazed that she would be interested in me but she was. Since I had no self-esteem and thought I was ugly, I couldn't understand why a smart, attractive, and sexy girl would talk to someone like me. I realized later that what I see in the mirror is not what others see and that is what it was with Katie. I had my first sexual encounter with Katie and we had as much fun as possible. I had no issues about my body when I was with her because she accepted me for what I was. In high school I always saw the popular boys and girls and wondered what it was like to be that way. To have people seek you out because you were attractive, smart, funny, or a good athlete. I never had to worry about that because I was not in that league then.

As time went on during my last two years of high school I always seemed to be fighting for everything I wanted because others said I could not do it or that it was not attainable. My stubbornness brought more ridicule each day. My high school teachers were brothers and lay teachers. Discipline was very strict and at times harsh and unwarranted.

One year I got into a disagreement with a student named Kevin. As we argued it escalated to a physical confrontation in class. Our instructor, Mr. Crutcher, came out of nowhere and hit me so hard I thought I had died. My mouth was swollen and I did not know what had happened. I only knew I was in deep shit. After my mother was called I went to the office to wait for her to pick me up. I was defending what this asshole had said about her and she was not happy with me. She said, "He should have hit you harder," meaning the teacher, because I was disrespectful to the instructor and class. This was a lesson to me but I also vowed to never back down from any adult or peer again. That pain of being hit was less than the emotional abuse I suffered each day.

Another kid in high school suffered the same fate as me at the hands of other kids. He was laughed at and made fun of because of his weight and lack of athletic ability. Gary had the heart of an angel. We never really spent time together in school but we knew each other. After high school we became as close as any two brothers could be.

We were different in many ways, and Gary was someone who I could talk to about anything and not be judged. Gary feared many things that I did not. I lived my life over the edge for many years and he was the reserved one. He lived through my adventures and I liked his stable lifestyle, one that I could not have. Our relationship soured after many years when Gary accused me of being a loser over a car deal we had. I had helped him with a nonprofit group to raise money for old cars being donated. I worked with him a short time and then needed a car. He let me take a Porsche for the work I had done and we set up a payment schedule that I could not keep. This put a strain on our friendship. I worked at trying to make the payments, but could not make them.

After a long period Gary and I spoke and he informed me he did not want to speak with me unless I had the money I owed him. He also added that I was a loser because of the way I lived my life, how I lied, cheated, slept with over 3,000 women, never worked, and always tried to get something over on others. This man was someone I loved because I felt accepted by him. I had no idea that all this anger toward me was present.

Years after we last spoke I found out he was arrested for embezzlement. Sad, but he could only see in me what he was and never was able to accept it. He has three wonderful and healthy children and a wife who is an angel. There are many times I miss him because we fought so many battles together, but people come into our lives for many reasons. I only think about the great times we had, what happened between us was meant to be, and I thank God for the time we had together. The one thing we were able to discuss was our body image issues because we had no one else to talk to about them.

We would talk for hours about size, muscles, what women want, eating right, and sexual issues around us hating our bodies when we were with women. To this day I have never had that freedom to share like this with another man.

During my senior year I started to feel better about myself and my body. I had gotten contacts my junior year and it helped to not feel so freakish with the thick black-rimmed glasses I wore. And girls were starting to notice me more and that was scary but oh so much fun!

I would go home at night and eat as much as possible because even though I felt better about myself I could not give up the one thing that I thought was the reason I felt better. Instead of eating so much in front of people I started to eat more alone and in silence.

I felt this great relief sitting in my room or car without someone watching me eat. I would park in places where no one could see me then throw the trash some place where no one would see me dump it. I was afraid to put it in trashcans because someone would know I was eating. At home, I put the wrappers under the bed or in a bag and then I would throw them away at school or elsewhere.

One day I had the courage to think that because I felt good, I would look at my body and see what the mirror had to show me. So I locked myself in mom's room and looked in a mirror at my naked body and I cried. I thought that it would look different, but in my mind it was fat and ugly. A rage built up inside that I cannot explain and I wanted to cut away the fat I saw staring back at me. I froze and could not move because I was afraid to feel the fat move with me. My breathing even made my body move and I tried holding my breath but it did not take away the ugly person I saw in the mirror. From that day on I always tried to avoid anything in which I could see my reflection. After this moment I ate McDonald's, Burger King, Carl's Junior. If I was disgusting, I might as well just keep eating.

I observed my family and there was no one like me at all. Everyone could get up from a meal and leave food; I could not. Why me? What was going on that I could not let food stay on the plate even when I was full? I realized that even then, when I got down to the last bite I was sad. I was losing the one thing that stopped my suffering. I felt as if my best friend was leaving me. I felt sad and lonely as I got close to the last bite of any meal.

The hate I had for my body sent me into many different directions trying to find answers that never existed because I had no idea what the hell I was doing to myself or why it was so important for my body to be perfect. It just was. I tried every diet there was that could help me according to the companies that make these life-threatening plans. Nothing worked. I tried soaps that remove fat, clothes that sweat off fat, pills that let you eat all you want and burn fat while asleep. It was a joke and I was a bigger joke for trying these methods.

My despair and hate for my body came to a crashing moment that I will never forget. One moment that I know a Higher Power controlled.

When I left home I had always lived by myself or with someone who I would not get to know very well so we would not spend time together. I wanted to isolate myself from everyone who could see me or judge me as I judge myself. I stayed isolated for years because I knew that people thought I was ugly and fat and I did not want them to see me this way.

I hated my body, so I knew everyone else did. I lived this way for over 30 years, until I realized that I had to make changes in my life that would allow me to deal with underlying issues of self-hate. I had to build a healthy lifestyle in order to get away from the distorted images I had of myself. And talking to others would be the first step when I was ready. I had this vision of what a perfect body was and it did not come from magazines, television, or sports. It came from the distorted world I lived in and created to deal with my emotional pain. I had never felt comfortable in my skin or having someone touch me, even though I used my body and sex to make money and support my food habit.

That one moment that I relive constantly happened in New York City. I had just moved there from California to model with Legends and had an agent named Leon McGraw. I was to be in town for a short time to get ready to head out to Japan with my buddy Jimmy.

I had been out all day and received a call from the booking agent that I had an audition at Bergdorf Goodman for a fashion show. I was dressed like a bum and had mustard stains on my shirt from lunch. I went as I was asked, knowing in my mind that they would not want me. With no portfolio, I headed over to meet with the representative and just headed home not thinking anything of it. As I headed home I called the agency and Leon informed me that I had booked the show. It was the first show in New York for Jean Paul Gautier. I was shocked and excited. It was being held downtown and the money was great for the little time I had to be there. All my fears came up big time that night. I was fat and ugly, so why did they choose me? But I needed the money and who knows who I could meet to have sex with after the show. I headed home to the roommate I was living with at the time. He was an addict like me, but his choices of drugs were heroin and alcohol. He had done a lot of modeling in Europe for many years and now wanted to act as well. It was a perfect fit, two addicts who never talked and allowed the other some personal space.

I was back stage with attractive people and I was just as good looking but did not believe it at that time. I did not belong and that was that. I sat there looking at others changing and I froze. I decided to change behind a small table, it wasn't much help but it did make me feel better. As the show went on we had little time to change and I knew no one would look, so I changed real fast.

Since I was getting paid I thought these people had really poor taste in choosing me so I was going to play for the pay. As I have always said, modeling had nothing to do with my eating disorder. I had all the issues way before this time in my life and it is just something I was lucky enough to do for a while and have fun making money. I have no blame for what I have been through and the entertainment industry is not responsible for me being sick or for the many others who suffer what I suffer from.

During the show I was on a high walking out knowing people were looking at me and I was eating it up. Once the show ended, the low started to creep in as it did every night. I avoided everyone I could and found a taxi to get me out of there. I had bought three dozen Mrs. Field's chocolate macadamia cookies that day and they were waiting for me at home in my closet. I stopped to get a quart of milk and then went home. As soon as I hit the door I was panicking. I was so embarrassed that people could have seen me and I felt guilt for taking the money to do the show when I felt I looked so pathetic. I sat down for a moment and then retrieved the cookies from the closet. I sat on the floor by the closet eating as fast as I could and drinking milk so I would not choke. With each bite the anxiety of the day and the pain I had in my head lessened.

As I ate the cookies I realized that everyone was lying to me and did not want to tell me how bad I looked. I knew in my head Leon got the show to do him a favor and book me. I got angry and violent to myself. I sat there, going over what I did in life that was good or bad. The bad far outweighed the good and I was tired of doing this every day. Tired of eating to cure my pain and stealing, prostituting myself, lying all the time and having sex with two or three different women each day to stop some of the pain. My body ached from the physical abuse I inflicted upon it. I was so tired, sad, lonely, and beyond depressed.

I stood up and slowly, with all the energy I had, took my clothes off. I had a mirror in the bedroom and stood before it trying to see what they saw in me when they hired me. I saw a disfigured man with no hope for a future because I could not stop eating and the body I had was horrible.

Knowing my roommate was out and would not be back until late or in the morning, I went into his room to look for the handgun he kept. He was paranoid about people being after him for reasons he never explained and I did not care to hear. I found the gun and took it back to my room, where I placed it next to the last two cookies I had not eaten. I was scared to live at this moment but more scared to die. I had wanted to do so much with my life but I was a burden on everyone who loved me or knew me. It was time to go and I knew it. I wanted to say goodbye, but I did not want to hear anyone's voice again.

The voice in my head was too much to overcome. I took five rounds of ammunition out of the revolver and placed them upright next to the cookies. I spun the barrel three times so that I could not see the chamber the last round was in. I have Obsessive-Compulsive Disorder and this was typical behavior for me. I had to do this my way even though it was crazy. I sat there for what seemed like hours just looking into space. I had no emotions left and I did not want to be a coward any more and cause others suffering because of the pain I could not stop.

I sat there laughing and crying in bursts. It felt as if I had left my body and was looking down on the person I hated the most and wanted to see suffer the most. I had a razor in the bathroom, which I brought into my room to help ease the emotional pain. I cut my arms, legs and face for that momentary relief I wanted. I hit the floor with my hands and face out of anger, shame, guilt and fear. I was getting more and more upset with myself and telling myself I needed to pick up the gun and stop being a sissy. Either do it or fucking go to bed, you coward, is all I heard in my head.

I had always wondered what it felt like to be God. To say whether someone lives or dies, but I never thought it would be me I was judging. I had loved the scene in "Deer Hunter" where they played Russian roulette. I played that scene over and over in my head for many years. Now it was my time to escape, but from what I still had no idea. My eyes were open and I watched in disbelief as I slowly pulled the trigger, wanting someone to stop me, but it was too late.

I had the gun at my temple because I was afraid if I put it in my mouth I would not die and then I'd live the rest of my life as a bigger burden to my family. As the trigger clicked I froze, no bullet. No bullet this time. I looked at myself and sweat covered my clothes, mixed with the blood from the abuse I inflicted earlier. I had cheated death in a game I saw in a movie. I felt as if I was somebody because I won. I played the ultimate game. How many of those bastards who hurt me would have the courage to try this. It was not courage, but a deep hatred for myself, and the body image I had of myself that night, that brought this moment to life.

I laid the gun down and felt as if I failed again at something. I placed the other rounds back in the gun and replaced it in my roommate's room. I came back and sat with the two cookies. I ate the cookies, laid down in my bed in a fetal position, and fell fast asleep. All this because I thought I was fat and ugly. By the way, my body fat was *eight percent* that day.

My life almost ended because I had what I now know to be a distorted body image. I thought that my body had betrayed me, but in reality I betrayed it by not getting help for my emotional issues that caused my dysfunctional view of me and my body. I still suffer physical pain from what I did to myself, a daily reminder that I never want to go there again.

My social life was nil, none, nada, because I was so paranoid about getting close enough to have somebody touch my body or see it. Even though I suffered from a sex addiction, I was in control and very few people ever saw my body. If they did, I made more money to compensate the emotional pain I would go through having them see me.

Each day was very exhausting trying to make up for the food abuse by abusing my body to make it look better to me. The hours spent in the gym trying to build the best body I could were wasted because I would use laxatives and food to soothe the emotional pain and then try to get rid of the calories I had consumed. My body was confused and so was I. Some days I felt great and my body was bloated and some days I felt like shit but my body was perfect in my distorted mind. While at the gym I would eat lunch on the bike or treadmill thinking I could burn the calories as soon as possible.

I would be so tired I would get up every morning and masturbate because I knew that my body was ugly and this was one way to get relief from the pain. Also, in my mind, it helped me get rid of the food I binged on the day before or even right before I went to the gym. I always thought that if I looked better then all the pain would go away. I was wrong; looking great does not cure any emotional pain. All the work I put into trying to look good caused more physical and emotional pain than the outcome.

You see, I thought that if by any chance I liked how I looked then someone else would see that confidence in me and like me. My personal sex life was hurt the most because I could not stand to have anyone touch me or even look at my body. Both of the women I lived with had no issues with my body, only I did. I always wanted to wear a shirt to bed so they could not see my stomach. When they would touch my stomach I would move their hands without ever telling them why, which caused them to question themselves at times. My issues had nothing to do with them, but I did not know how to tell them. I thought that they would be turned off if they saw me completely naked. I was wrong but I never realized that then.

Having sex for money was a thrill and exciting to me because of the power and control. I never realized that I was paid to leave, not to stay. The high was unfathomable to me. I felt bad sometimes, not because I was getting paid, but because I did not look as I wanted and it made me feel like I was stealing their money. However, I earned it and more. Sex has nothing to do with the body; it all starts in the mind and goes from there. My mind has no equal and what I did for the money made everything worth it to all my clients.

In early 1994 I went to see my therapist in Oakland, California. Not only was she beautiful, she understood eating disorders and that men suffer as women do. She was the first therapist who took the time to help me and not judge me. I liked seeing her and listening to her. The serenity I felt when I was with her was the best. This day my mom and friend took me for my appointment and I was really in bad shape. My body was so swollen that when I walked my legs rubbed together and that mortified me. I was not the best person to be with, but my mom and friend stayed with me to help.

I didn't want to see my therapist that day for no other reason than I had to climb stairs to see her and it would be so traumatic for me. I was scared and ashamed at the same time. I had a hard time breathing when I was sitting down. I begged my mom to find a parking spot near the door and she did the best she could. I was so scared people would see me sweating and dressed with so many clothes on that they would think something was wrong. Well, something was wrong and if anybody knew the building they knew all the occupants were therapists. My paranoia was in high alert that day.

There were sixteen steps from the bottom to the top with people coming and going all the time. I wanted to find a back way in, but there was only one way in and one way out. It hurt to breathe and I hated the fact that I looked so fat and gross. Each breath felt as if my skin would burst and with each step I heard the sound of an elephant in my head as my feet hit the ground. I had tears in my eyes but I did not cry because I did not want anyone to see a grown man crying on the sidewalk. That would have crushed me even more. It seemed as if it took forever to get inside but it was only about ten minutes.

As I stood at the bottom all I could feel was disgust, shame, and guilt for being this needy of my mom and friend and for having the problems I had. I panicked and began to sweat like I had just taken a bath. My climb took almost two hours because of my fear and the fact that I froze after each step. I had two angels with me and they did nothing but support me each horrible step of the way. Even though I felt my stomach juggle with each step and heard the pounding of an elephant, I made it. My vision was blurred this day and my pulse was running a marathon. But, I made it and was so proud of myself because I had wanted to give up and go home the whole trip. I had my meeting with the therapist and it went great. When we left it took no time to get downstairs and out to a restaurant to eat. That was my reward for making it to the therapist. Even though my mom and friend said we should go home I manipulated them to do what I wanted. Nothing ever stopped me from getting my way. Nothing.

In my mind, my body was my canvas and I the artist. Every time I did see myself in a reflection or mirror I wondered what I could do or what I was not doing to better my body so that I would be disgusted each time I saw myself. It was exhausting trying to hide from any reflection of myself in private or in public. When I did see the reflection I would panic and swear to myself that what I saw was disfigured and ugly. I would then think of what I needed to do to get to the body that I knew lived under all this fat and disfigurement.

The person I saw in the mirror had a large protruding stomach, even though I had defined abs. My face was puffy and fat even though my face had great definition. My legs were so big because I could feel them rub against each other when I walked and this disgusted me to no end. My waist was the worst, even though I had a 29-31 inch waist, it always seemed much bigger. I could always tell if my body had gained weight by closing my thumb and index finger around my wrist. If it had room it was good, if not I panicked. I always thought that others saw what I felt, but no one ever did. The suffering I went through to hide from people was my own making.

Many times the only way to deal with the loser I saw in reflections was to punch myself all over my body to take the emotional pain away. I knew where physical pain came from, but not the emotional pain. I had no idea where to start to stop it. Eating, sex and physically hurting myself relieved me from everything, but only for short periods of time. The physical abuse I suffered at my own hands has never gone away. I have numbness in my arms, hands and legs all the time. I cannot sleep at night because my hands always fall asleep. I have had two surgeries for temporal-mandibular joint problems and my jaw sounds like a breaking bone each time I open my mouth. The pain and headaches are nothing I would wish on an enemy. I lost 80 percent of the feeling in my face from the surgeries and it has slowly come back over the years. I do not have it all back yet. I cannot really taste things unless I add something sweet because my nerves were severed for over eight hours during my first surgery.

With each bite or spoken words, the cracking of the bone sends sharp pains to the left side of my face. When I wake up in the morning it takes a while to be able to open my mouth completely because if I do it too quickly it feels as if my face will burst. My body feels the constant bruising from throwing myself into walls to cure the emotional pain I was suffering at that moment. My head has soft spots that hurt when I touch them, caused by slamming my head against anything when I was angry, depressed, or frustrated. These are not healthy coping skills and please do not try them. But this is the only way I knew at the time to take the pain away.

My cycle of fixing what I thought was wrong with me never ended. Once I saw myself I would begin my plan to change myself physically. I would lay out carefully how I would change the body parts I did not like. I tried every diet I could find and created my own. DIET to me now stands for **D**angerous **I**dentity **E**nhancing **T**rap. When I dieted to cure my emotional needs I deprived myself for long periods of time and then when I thought I had done good, the first thing I did was eat what I had stopped eating as a reward. The cycles would start again. The parent punishes the child, then rewards the child when the child corrects whatever he or she was punished for. I was my own parent, punishing and rewarding myself at the same time.

In 1994 I was living in San Francisco, constantly looking for that quick fix to lose weight without having to do anything. The less energy I had to put out, the better I felt about it. I knew in my sick mind I would keep going until I found the solution to all my problems by changing my body to fit my dysfunctional views. I found the cure in a health food store one day and knew my life would change. I bought the sauerkraut program and was ready to make this my last diet to get it right. What I was trying to get right I had no idea. The directions were easy enough and being the addict I was I thought I would do the program a little longer because I would lose more weight. Sounded logical to me. Even Mr. Spock would agree with me, Captain Kirk.

Since I lived in my own world they knew I had good reasons for trying things my own way. I had to take the drink of sauerkraut juice three times a day for three days. I did it three times a day for 10 days. I drank this and water for 10 straight days and had nothing else. Now if you like sauerkraut, I was the person to be around. If not, you did not want to be within 20 feet of me because it was coming out my pores in a flood. Everywhere I went people would walk away or comment on the smell, that smell being me. Needless to say it did not work and I have never eaten sauerkraut again in my life. I was so desperate I would try anything. All I ever lost was money and time and a piece of my mind.

I really knew I was overboard after I met with two sure-fire weight loss specialists, at least that's what they said they were. I scheduled a meeting with a Jenny Craig representative in Southern California in 1994 for a consultation. At this time my body fat was around nine percent, but I thought I needed to lose more weight in order to feel good about me. I arrived 20 minutes before the meeting. I am never late for anything. I was escorted into a small room by a very professional young woman and waited for the rep to start the consultation. Within a few minutes a thin and somewhat attractive lady entered and started reviewing what I had told the initial contact about why I wanted to start Jenny Craig. She did not even take a breath and without asking me for any reasons about why I wanted to lose weight, she said I could lose up to 15 pounds for my body and lower my body fat percentage.

I weighed 170 pounds at this time and, in reality, I could not lose another pound. This was my salvation, a place that does not really care what happens to me and will feed into my dysfunctional needs and take the credit. The woman was great, she told me what I wanted to hear, not the truth. I walked out and really thought about it, but decided they were not a place that I could trust. They preyed on my weakness and never once asked any questions that could have sent up a red flag. I left there angry and sad that once again I failed to find something that could help. I do not blame them for any of my problems, but they feed off people like me who have no hope and are willing to die to lose weight.

My second meeting took place in 1995, after trying so hard to get better, but nothing was working. I had bloated to 275 pounds and since I wore baggy clothes, no one ever noticed but me. I hated myself for all this weight and I had been only 170 pounds less than a year before.

My shame and disgust led me to a plastic surgeon. I met with him in Los Angeles to discuss what he could do and what I would look like after. I hated needles and hospitals, but I was willing to try anything at this time. After we spoke I realized the money it would cost would take away from food, so I decided against it. I wanted him to cut out so much of my body that he thought I was crazy, and, well, I was. I had wanted to have my stomach, legs, arms, and face liposuctioned because I felt so fat and ugly. My paranoia had nothing to do with what other people looked like. I had no issues with other people's bodies; it was just mine I hated.

Since I did not have the operations, I went back to another sure-fire remedy that I knew would not be healthy, but it made me feel better about the lack of control I had with food and I could lose weight as well. I started slowly but built up to around 300 laxatives a day in less than a week. I had taken laxatives for many years and stopped at times because I did not need them. I hated that they made me tired and dehydrated, but nothing else could help me as they did. I started spending six hours a day at the gym and eating less than 1,500 calories. In less than three months I had dropped to 190 pounds. My body was so out of whack that it was used to the weight shifts and the trauma I had inflicted upon it. It seemed so easy to just pop the pills before, during, and after a meal, but the physical damage was costly.

I had no idea when I would have to go to the bathroom, and it would hit me at the most inappropriate times – at work, during sex, on a bus or subway, or during a meeting. If a bathroom was not available, I made a toilet in public places. Because I could not control my bowels at night, I sometimes would soil my sheets, and the emotional pain and embarrassment of this moment kept me frozen and ashamed. I would lie there paralyzed and numb, not being able to move. The smell would be so bad that I would lie there and vomit on myself, but I still could not move.

After I stopped using the laxatives it took my body over one year to be able to regulate itself again to have bowel movements normally without the help of laxatives. These memories are as fresh in my mind today as when they happened. I never forget anything that I did to myself with the hope that it will never happen again.

In early 1994, after I had failed to maintain the bar my brother Richard and I had opened in Thornton, California, I was in my apartment in San Francisco and had sunk to my lowest depth of paranoia and fear since my first stay in rehab. I was so scared that people would see me and judge me like I judged myself that I did what I could to feel safe from that shame. I made my apartment reflection proof and went from living on top of the furniture to living on the floor like an animal. I had every mirror, doorknob, all my silverware, windows, shower doors and showerhead, microwave, toaster, refrigerator handle and even my television covered. I was even afraid to see my reflection in my shadow, so I wrapped towels around my stomach to keep it flat just in case I saw it by mistake. It made it hard to breathe, but easier to deal with my body if I had the unpleasant chance of seeing it.

I kept the place dark day and night. I put large black curtains over the windows and used a staple gun to keep any light from coming in. I didn't even want anyone to see me through the windows. Sadly, I lived on the third floor so in reality no one could see me, but I thought at that time neighbors across the street would look at me through their windows.

I had sunk so low that the monster I had become in my head at this time now wanted out. I wanted to make it all go away and this time it was not by killing myself. I knew I needed to reach out for help, but who could or would help me? That was the problem. I knew from my past attempts that it cost a lot of money and that no one really helped men. But I did find the right place to set me on my journey to recovery.

It took more than three years to really gain confidence in my body issues and reduce the harsh opinion I had of my physical appearance. I had many good days and some bad days, but I built really good coping skills and had really good, healthy people around me who really cared, and I let them care for the first time in my life. I felt I did not have to do it all alone as I had before.

Chapter Four: Somebody Please Help Me!

Some time in the late 1980s in New York City, I was tired, depressed, sad, angry, and hungry. I had been up all night trying to come to terms with the fact that I was not going to get any help for whatever it was that caused me to eat all the time and throw up the food after every meal. I was angry with myself, because I always thought I could take care of whatever problems I faced because I had all the answers. The night before I had sat and done what I did best to take away the emotional pain: I ate food and banged my fists and head against the wall to take away the pain in my head, my typical ritual when in a stressful mood. I had tried to understand what was wrong with me and I could not. What did I have, and what, if anything, could someone else do? I had never heard of anyone else acting like this, and I thought it was just normal because it was what had I done for so many years. Now it was really hard to deal with on a day-to-day basis. I did not want to admit defeat, but I needed someone else to tell me what the hell was happening.

I sat in my apartment calling medical doctors, therapists, psychiatrists, and even hospitals. No one would or could help me. I told them my symptoms and that a therapist in California said I had an eating disorder. They did not understand what I was talking about, and if they did they informed me that men do not suffer from what my symptoms seemed to reveal. Out of the 42 telephone calls I made that day, only three got any response and it was not what I needed to hear. Each one said my symptoms sounded like I had an eating disorder. They had treated some women in the past, but never a man because from what they knew this only affected women. I had symptoms for an illness that only women are supposed to have and what in the hell was I to do?

I sat there frozen in time, as if the world had stopped and nothing moved. I heard my heart beat faster and faster and then the telephone rang. Even though I could hear the voice on the answering machine, I did not pick up because I could not move. I had these moments all the time and just waited for them to pass. Sometimes they passed quickly; sometimes it took hours to move again. After I was able to function I retrieved the message. It was from one of the three offices that understood eating disorders. The caller informed me that she had called around to see if anyone worked with men who suffered from this and the answer jolted me out of my seat.

The one doctor she was able to reach had worked with men who suffered eating disorders. I sighed with relief and she stopped for a moment and said that all his cases were men who were obese or young gay men. These were the only men he had seen suffering from this new illness. Well, I was not gay or obese at that time and I wondered whether or not it would do any good to talk to him. Since I had no hope, I spoke with him on the telephone. The doctor was very polite and adamant that I must have been sexually abused as a child or confused about my sexuality if I did have an eating disorder. He explained that this was a woman's disease and that gay men had so many emotional problems and connections with women, it was easy for them to have this illness. Men do not have body image issues as women do, he explained. Men do not have the emotional needs that women have in order to feel good about who they are. Men are more apt to have drug or drinking problems. This is what this man told me. He also said I should look at the DSM3 to see what the symptoms are for bulimia and I would see that it was not my problem.

After we spoke I went to the library and checked the DSM3 for eating disorders. I fit the description perfectly. Here was a doctor who said he treated only gay men who suffered because their emotional make-up was like a woman and obese men because it was obvious they had problems. But he could not help someone like me. That was the end of that. I was scared and depressed. I knew I had a disease that everyone said was only for women and gay or obese men. No one would help me, so I had to help myself.

At this time I knew I was on my mom's insurance, so I called them to ask for help. They would not even give me a referral because they said they did not treat eating disorders and the only people with those symptoms were women. I called my mother to help and it took a lot to convince her to help me out. I could not understand why so many professionals who pride themselves on treatment and specialize in different modalities would not help me. They did help women, but would not take a man because it was something they said men didn't suffer from.

Once the insurance company agreed to help me, I called treatment centers for eating disorders, but no one treated men. My first two stays in treatment were at places that had not treated men but they took a chance to try and help me. They failed.

I

Soon I entered an eating disorder clinic in Concord, California, for the first treatment stay of what would ultimately be three attempts to deal with my problems. My therapist told me my issues were deeply rooted and the eating disorder, sex addiction, gambling, self-mutilation, and other compulsive behaviors were coping skills I used rather than dealing with the problems head on. My eating disorder was the primary issue and I needed to get that under control because I turned to everything else to relieve the pain I suffered from the eating disorder.

The facility director informed me that she knew men suffered from eating disorders and they had not treated anyone like me before. I told her I needed help or I was going to die from this, so we set up a meeting and if all went well I would be admitted that day. When I walked in to see her I was taken back by her size. She was 5'4" tall and weighed at least 280 pounds. The first thing I thought was this is crazy and I wanted out of there. She was kind and understanding; we spoke about the program and what I had to do. While we talked I thought I would probably gain weight while in the center because she was the director and so large. That frightened me.

She told me she sensed something was on my mind and asked me if I wanted to talk. I told her I didn't want to appear rude, but how could she help me if she was so big. She explained that the difference between us was that she had learned to love herself for who she was and not what she looked like and I hated who I was. I sat there for a moment and began to cry. She was right. I entered the facility that day and for the next 20 days it was a roller coaster ride and a challenge for them and for me.

Dr. Holtzman was the psychiatrist assigned to me. She told me I had to really work on things and share in groups and to take my medications. I felt nervous but open. After two weeks it was very difficult because the only person I thought understood men was my therapist and we talked on the telephone. I saw her maybe once during my visit there. I rebelled against some groups and a yoga class, so the doctor came to visit me one day. He told me if I did not get better I was going to be a loser like I had been for the rest of my life. He was very judgmental about my past and what I had done to survive. With this type of doctor, who the hell had a chance? The other staff members were helpful, but didn't really understand me, and some of the women didn't want a man in the group.

One week before I left on my own – because I knew I was cured – we had visiting hours and a friend came to see me. She checked in and came straight to my room. I thought this was odd, but no one said anything. We were not allowed visitors in the rooms unless they were family. Since I was the only man the attendants never really checked on me when I had visitors, so my friend and I had sex right there in my room. I thought that, if they were not going to care, I would do as I wanted. I had 12 days left on insurance and then the help would stop. After those 12 days, I was back out in full force with my addiction and living hell. I was to blame for my problems, but this rehab center didn't have the knowledgeable staff to help a man.

II

In early 1994, I was set to enter a rehab center for eating disorders in Redwood City near San Francisco. We had everything worked out and I was going to be there 45 days. I felt so much relief and excitement knowing I was not going to be in control all the time and that someone really knew how to treat men. Things didn't turn out the way I planned. Before I went in I had my last meal. It was so gross and disgusting, that should have cured me. I always had last meals and they last over 30 years.

I arrived on a Thursday and was informed that I would not see a primary therapist until Monday. I was upset, but at least I was there. Then they told me I could eat whatever I wanted for the next four days until the nutritionist came on Monday. Now I was scared, but I hung in there. What kind of place was this? I found out on Friday night. The only food I ate was popcorn with Tabasco® sauce and this disgusting drink called Ensure®. It is given to those who need to gain weight and I did not. Friday night I found out that this place really was a psych unit and treated very few eating disorder clients and that, because it was having financial problems, I was going to be released on Monday with everyone else.

I was devastated. They had to have known this was possible before I came in. No one would answer any questions and on Monday I left. I ate over $200 in food at a nearby Denny's Restaurant and, with each bite, the pain of the past four days went away.

In these first two tries I felt like a guinea pig. Each clinic wanted the money and would say anything to get me in, and it worked. Prior to going into treatment I had so many diagnoses that I had no idea who I was or what could be done. I was diagnosed with depression, obsessive-compulsive disorder, attention deficit hyperactivity disorder, borderline personality disorder, narcissistic personality disorder, and avoidant personality disorder. I had more personalities, it seemed, than Sybil from the movie – and I was told this when the professionals said I did not have an eating disorder. I did not want to be a guinea pig any more and said, to hell with these people – I will cure myself. You can imagine how good I was at that.

III

I entered my last rehab facility in July, 1994, in southern California. I had searched for a place and this was the one that was able to treat me. They understood men who suffered from eating disorders. I was an inpatient for 52 days and the treatment worked, thanks to some of the staff and two administrators.

When I arrived I was one of two men with 16 women. I let it be known that I was there for me and not there to help others. One thing many of us do when we go into rehab is try to cure others so we do not have to deal with our own issues. It was fun, frustrating, empowering, honest, and what I needed. Some of the staff had a problem with a male in the groups and they did not have a problem letting me know. The women I had the pleasure to meet in there were all suffering from the same illness but used different methods to heal their pain. Some of the other patients and I still speak from time to time. It was great to hear others share their lives and I related to what they felt. This was a good place for me. It was the start of my recovery, which took until 1997 to really have a structured foundation.

Until this stay I had seen eight different professionals who tried to help me and at the same time only two who knew how to work with someone who suffered from eating disorders. I had to stay in centers that did not work and had tried countless times to cure myself. I was at my ropes' end when this opportunity came about. Prior to this stay, I tried everything to treat my illness after I spoke with the professionals I had seen. One therapist asked me to outline my daily habits and I did. It was nothing for me to wash my hands three hundred times a day, over and over until they were raw. I would lock and unlock my door ten times every time someone entered my apartment. I would place everything in order so no one could touch it without my knowing about it. I counted things in fives all day long and would start over so many times I lost three or four hours a day sometimes just sitting and counting things.

Since I was all these different things, or so the professionals said, and couldn't find help, I decided to use them to my advantage whenever I was questioned about my lifestyle. Since I was labeled as the one who was sick in the family, I might just as well be sick. These labels helped me out of so many situations, but I also used them to hurt and use others so I could feel good at that time. I could not heal the eating disorder, so I took it out on those who loved me and those I did not even know.

The biggest obstacle I faced in my efforts to get help was that there was very little, if any, research done on men when I was sick. To this day there is still very little. Those facilities I reached out to did not treat men because many think we do not suffer as women do from this disease. Is this right? No. But we need to keep pushing the medical profession to help us and to create guidelines for those who want to treat patients so we know they are making a difference.

Chapter Five: My Blame Game

God damn it, all I need is $500.00. It's not a lot. I mean you spend it on cigarettes every month. No, no, don't do that. Don't ask me what I need it for because I just need it. Yeah, you gave me money last week – so what? Okay, all right. I need it for rent and I did not want you to worry. Please, I'm wasting time just sitting here. They need the money today or I am out. Is that what you want? You don't care, do ya? Fuck it. Forget about it. It's no big deal.

I paused, knowing that she would still be there, because she never hung up and always took the abuse I gave.

Fuck, you don't get it, do you. I have no food, no money, no car, and I am going to lose the only place I have to live. You know what? I don't need your money and I don't want it.

Suddenly I hung up the phone, sat counting in my head to 30, and then called back. I apologized and lied more, knowing that my mom would soon say "yes" and I would have the money I needed to eat and waste on anything other than what I had told her it was for.

I didn't care what she might have been going through at that moment. It was all about me and only me. I knew that if I was nice and acted helpless I would get her to feel bad and as if she had done something wrong. I always made everyone feel as if they where the reason I was sick or in trouble or stealing to survive. I asked again, "Well, what do you think?" And she stopped me in mid-sentence. She said she could push her bills back and had enough food to eat that week, and I did not care – I just wanted the money. She said she would send me the money and it would be at Western Union in half an hour. She sent $1,000, so I could have extra money to eat with and pay bills.

What she did not know was that I had no apartment and was living with a friend and had no bills. I needed the money to eat and pursue my sex addiction. I always told her never to tell my brother, so, if I spoke to him, he would help me, too. I played on the two most important people's love for me to feed my dysfunctional lifestyle. Since I did not live near them they never knew the truth and, if they did, they always helped my no matter what they sacrificed. I victimized them as I did many others at this time.

I blamed everyone who hurt me in my past and allowed that hate and anger to vent toward my family, because I knew they loved me and would always take care of me no matter what. Since I hated myself and was afraid to try and do anything, because I looked so bad and was fat and ugly in my head, I would make them feel as if my problems were all because of family issues and the past. I was not strong enough to take care of myself because I did not know how. It was always someone else's fault why I had no job or could not pay bills. I found someone or something to blame for my failure as a man to take care of myself. I used every excuse I could, even the deaths of my grandmother and sister-in-law, for not being able to cope with life.

I knew each time I picked up the phone that my illness was getting the best of me, but I could not reach out for help because everyone would say I was using my illness to manipulate everything and not be responsible for my life or the trauma I brought onto others.

If it was not my family, I would seek out others who were like me but weaker, and dominate the relationships until I got what I needed. If things where not working out or I was not pulling my share I made sure I convinced them that they were the problem, not me. It made it easier to manipulate people because they were not responsible for their lives. So, I took responsibility for them. They thought I cared and I may have, but I used them until it was time to move on. If the relationship ended, I would always tell them it was their fault and they were to blame. No one ever saw me coming and when I left it was over. We fed each other's illnesses, and I always chose them for what I could get. They were easy targets who already had issues and believed they were to blame for other people's problems – so why not mine?

I was always so sure that I had all the answers to everyone's problems because it allowed me to not deal with my own issues. In my mind, my reality was so warped that I could take positive criticism toward me and turn it around, so the person who said it to me would be blamed for whatever I did, based on that person trying to help me, that was dysfunctional.

As food became my reward for everything I did – good or bad – I was able to see what I was doing at the time, but could not stop. I knew of nothing – at least nothing that made me feel this good – that would help me through my pain other than my compulsive behaviors and blaming others for what should have been my responsibility. The people I blamed for my problems were never the problem. I was. They might have been part of the problem, but a very small part. Because I was so set on not dealing with reality and the truth, I used others to cure the pain. As long as I was rescuing them, they owed me – and how dare they not see that what I was trying to do was for them, not me. I wore blinders like a horse in a race. I could not see anything other than what was in front of me, and it was not healthy at all.

So many times I would find a job and quit before anything ever went bad. I am sure, now, I could have done all those jobs, but I did not want to work or take orders from anyone. Everything had to fit my time frame during the day or it was some reason other than the truth why I could not do it.

I used to blame whoever wrote the daily horoscopes, because it was their fault that I did not have a productive day. I read what I wanted to see, and it made each day easier to stay unfocused and unproductive. All this time my concentration was on getting food and sex, and the other behaviors that eased my pain. Anything for food, anything.

Once I entered recovery, I learned that the easiest way for me to get better was to be honest. I had to be honest with me first before I could with anyone else. It was hard and painful to admit what I had done out of fear and anger to others and myself. Once I did this, and it was a slow process because of my past coping skills, it was always a struggle about how I could be responsible and accountable for what I had done and would do in my life.

At times I thought about possibilities. But that did not help. I could only deal with the here-and-now, and the reality is I have today, not yesterday or tomorrow. Today I make a difference, so that tomorrow I can benefit from what I did today.

I always wanted someone to admit their mistakes or to say they were sorry to me. But, now I say I am sorry and I mean it, and it is the truth. To say I was wrong or sorry for what I did to people, even though they hurt me, is the greatest relief I can have. No one ever made me act as I did. Yes, I was very ill ninety percent of the time, but the times I was aware I still acted wrong and out of line.

My growth as a person started the day I was able to admit to myself the type of person I had been and see that the type of person I wanted to be was within my ability as a person and a man. If I have a bad day today, I look at what took place and what my part was in the situation. I look at what could have been done, instead of finding reasons to blame someone else. If I choose to let others in my life, now I know the pros and cons of who they are, the positives and negatives they bring into my life and vice versa, what they are about. I do not blame them, because it takes two to make things happen.

I am responsible for my life today and it is not easy, but it gets easier every day. There is no magic to make my past go away. It is a part of me and I grow from it everyday. To forget my past would take away from the person I am today, and I love me more than I ever thought I could or would. Hell, I even like me.

I wrote *The Daily Process: 16 Points to Life*© while in my last inpatient stay in 1994, and I read them and implement them in my life every day. They are different from twelve-step programs because they are not God based. I wrote them because I needed something more than what was out there. These *Points* helped me become accountable and responsible, through something I had never had. That something was self-nurturing. Like you, I have the answers to my problems, but need something to guide me, and these *Points* guide me everyday, as does THE NUTRITION & BODY IMAGE PROGRAM™ that got me through my eating disorder with *The 16 Points*. More on these later.

I now have less stress on my heart, mind, body, and soul because I choose to be honest and accept my part in what I do and say. I still make choices that could be better, but I learn from the mistakes now. The best thing is, I do not turn to my past for the answers now. I use the new tools I have to find solutions.

Chapter Six: What Is a Man?

If I had listened to the many people who tried to tell me what made a man when I was growing up, I would be a 250 pound, beer drinking, jeans-wearing, macho, womanizing, Sunday morning armchair quarterback asshole. Someone who does not cry at movies, always solves women's problems (I have learned that women want a man to listen, not solve their problems), is the breadwinner, and does not want the wife to work. When I was a child, people who described a man made it very scary to want to grow up. From childhood, my mom, the teachers at Holy Cross grade school, and then the coaches in high school taught me men do not show emotion. My uncles were the only real male models I had until grade school, and each of them had some problems that sure as hell made me want not to be the men they were.

I am glad that I never used these people or relatives as examples of how to be a man. I cry at movies, even when I am alone; it feels good. I feel emotional pain and ask for help. I don't drink, but that is a boy's passage to manhood in many families and communities – and that is scary. I listen to advice from women on everything I do, and I hear what they are saying. Being a man does not make me any better than women, or weak because I share my feelings. I never played football in high school, or sat around telling other men about my sexual conquests. My best friend is my mom. So, what is a man? A man is whatever you want to be. Labels only do one thing, and that is prevent men and women from growing intellectually, spiritually, and emotionally as individuals and partners in life.

Growing up and throughout my life, I have faced many questions concerning my personal likes and dislikes. I am proud that I have never defended my likes and dislikes, because they are just that – mine. Many people tend to negate someone else as a person if they do not understand them or their life choices. From the clothes we wear to the people we date, so many people think they have the answers because their life is working for them. At least, they think this. I faced a lot of ridicule in grade school and high school, because my mom was always there by my side at everything I did. Well, I did not have a dad. My mom, grandmother, and great-grandmother did a great job being mom and dad to my brother and me.

Having a mother who made more sacrifices than the fathers of the kids I grew up with, to be at our games, practices, and school events, drew harsh comments from the other kids. I was called sissy, fag, queer, momma's boy, loser and more. These comments, because I knew no better at that time, made me draw away from mom because I did not want to be shamed like this for being who I was. My mom did nothing wrong, but I wanted friends and thought if I backed away from mom I would have them. It only strained my relationship with my mom, and I was wrong to do that. She had done nothing, but I thought she had. I wanted to be accepted, and hurt the person who was my best friend; it was never right.

One thing I was very fortunate to receive from my mom was the permission to feel what I wanted and express what I needed at any time. At times that was confusing, because she would yell at me to be a man when she never told me what a man was. Hell, I was just learning to tie my shoes and spell my name. Being a man when I was a boy was not something I was ready to do.

I wonder to this day what my life would have been like if I had a dad, and what I would have learned from him about being a man. People have always asked me what it was like to grow up without a father and if I missed him. To be honest, if you never have something, how do you know what it is like to miss it? That was my justification when I was younger to deal with the pain of having no father in my life. Later, I realized the huge void in my life without a father. I was very lucky by the grace of God to be raised by three very strong, independent, wonderful, and nurturing ladies. I would not have traded those ladies for any father in the world. There is a reason for everything in life, and it is hard at times to believe this. I know there was a reason I had no father, and I had to learn to deal with what I was given – and I was given the world with these ladies. The gifts I learned each day from watching these ladies are worth their weight in gold. My passions in life come from them. My compassion for others was their compassion for me. My ability to nurture myself, even though it took years, comes from the nurturing I received as a child.

Through all the emotional hell I have been through because I have never fit the mold as the typical male, I know that others make their choices because they are afraid to change. Men do not want to be seen as weak, and will say and do things they think they are supposed to do to be accepted by both other men and women. In our society we always hear that men pressure women to look as they want them to look for their own self gratification, and that is true. I have also met many women who are willing to ridicule a man if he is not like good old dad, or if he does not have the right job, car, house, money, or body. Each gender prevents the other from just being who they are, because we have been taught that men have one role in life and women have another. I know that men and women can do the same things, and that if they would just stop labeling each other both genders would find an inner serenity they have not known. When people try to be something they are not, it only creates more dysfunction in a world that is not easy to live in for anyone.

I have learned that, through my emotions and feelings, I have grown not only as a person but as a man. I am a better son, brother, and lover because I accept who I am and do not try to be what others want me to be for their own needs. Just as my food habits started as a child, so did my observations on men and women. Even though there were no men in the house, my mom and grandmothers never disparaged men or my father to my brother or me. They never said that cooking and cleaning were for women and that men had to do the yard and fix everything around the house. I lived with my second girlfriend, named Carla, who could build anything with a power saw and landscape a house with no problems. Me, hell, I would hit my thumb every time I tried for the nail, and I hated fixing anything in the apartment. She was able to fix the house up and build things because she learned how – as many people do – from her parents. How parents view the opposite gender and each other is how many kids view the opposite gender in their own lives.

I had the chance when young to question anything, without being ridiculed or told that was not for me to ask.

My mom tried to answer everything she could and not to pass judgment on my brother and me.

Home is where everything starts and then branches out. If a young man is taught he cannot ask for help, or sees his dad holding everything inside, then there is a great possibility he will do the same thing as an adult. We learn from our parents many traits, some good and some bad. This is not a blame game, but the truth. What we learn from them was passed on down from their parents and grandparents. Parents have to pay attention to what they tell their children, and keep their children's best interests in mind when making decisions. Sharing their beliefs is great, but to degrade a child because the child has different ideas on roles in life from what mom and dad have planned for them is simply wrong. If mom and dad define a child by gender, that child will use what the child thinks he or she is supposed to be, instead of who he or she is, to achieve things in life. Role-playing can be fun, depending on the situation and need. But if we play the man who is the boss and women play the helpless person as some are taught, then we have a future that allows for no personal growth and does not hold us accountable for our thoughts, ideas, actions, and behaviors. We can always blame someone else, because that is how we were taught to be as men and women.

Men and women fear loneliness, isolation, being shamed, degraded, being judged, financial issues, lack of education, job security, health issues, growing old, sexual problems, raising kids, faith, family issues, and not being good enough or loved. This is just a small list, but we all worry about these things, and, as well, we like the same things in life. We just don't communicate, because we are told to keep emotions separate. We think if we do not talk about our fears they will disappear. They won't disappear, and ignoring our difficulties makes them worse. I worry about all these things because what effect will they have on my life when I face these situations? Will I be able to handle them in a healthy way? I worry, but I do not think as a man I have to do it one way or another. I have to figure out what is best for me.

When I first got sick, it was a nightmare when doctors and therapists told me only women have eating disorders. They would not even return phone calls because I was a man, and many of the therapists I spoke with told me I must have been abused sexually or that I had to be gay. I mentioned this in Chapter Four. I called for support groups and had other professionals tell me that they did not know of any groups that men could attend to discuss their issues or problems, because men don't really have eating disorders.

I have learned that more men in life will work with a so-called life coach rather than a therapist because they do not want people to think they need help. My roller coaster ride has continued with therapists and eating disorder facilities since I have been in recovery. Some places tell me that they have a program for men, but the truth is they have no idea how to work with men, nor do they understand the differences between men and women who have eating disorders.

In 1997, I went to Washington, D.C., to meet with Members of Congress and representatives of the Health and Human Services Department. Many of the politicians I met gave me the run-around: They said they would be interested in helping put together a bill to help those who suffered from eating disorders, but they needed someone else to take the lead first. I met with men and women in Congress and those who work with the insurance industry. All of them were shocked that I was a man who suffered from this disease. Even though they knew very little, they thought it was for women only. The National Institute for Mental Health's guidelines for someone who suffered from anorexia are listed as "A 17-25-year-old Caucasian female, middle to upper class." This was their definition for this disease in 1997. It was a joke, and it also showed me that politicians, unless they have something to gain, will not put their necks on the line.

While I was in Washington, a bill being was being passed that would help those who suffer from eating disorders, but it did not include men. I fought and argued for many months and they changed the wording to say, "... for all those who suffer other than women ...". What the hell, did they mean animals or what? No one wanted to add men to this list. During my trip I met with organizers of a national program to bring education and awareness on eating disorders and body image to young girls throughout the country, and they would not include this material for boys. It was about 'girl power,' and that was what they were going to do. Women and girls do need this information, but men and boys need it as well.

One meeting with a senior medical doctor and other women in the women's department of health turned into an argument from the moment I walked in the door. The women I met wanted to know why I was there to discuss eating disorders, as I was a man. They said that research on all major illnesses up to that time had been on men, and that the only real research for women was for eating disorders. I was appalled, and explained to them that they were mothers and grandmothers. I asked them how would they feel if the men in their families had nowhere to turn for help. It took two months of constant telephone calls, but we built a good relationship. The people I met in Washington wanted to help just girls and women, and down the line they would consider boys and men. To this day, when it comes to eating disorders, there is very little help provided to or research done on men and boys.

Eating disorders know no color, race, religion, faith, economic background – or gender. I did not choose to be a man with an eating disorder, even though I do not regret it. It has changed my life in many ways, and allowed me to reach others who are suffering. I am not the freak that many men and women have told me I was because I have an eating disorder. I turned to food to soothe the pain I suffered. The eating disorder had nothing to do with gender.

I was afraid to discuss my eating disorder and other issues for many years because I was a man and did not even know where to turn for help. I lost so much during that time that I will never gain back, but I have no regrets now. I knew that people would question my sexuality and laugh at me for having what most consider a woman's disease. I am proud of the courage I have displayed in light of the prejudices I faced from medical professionals and non-professionals even to this day. I am not alone, and there are many men and women who suffer every day. They are courageous and loving people who need help, and do not need to be chastised for an illness they cannot control.

During my last stay in rehab, in 1994, I was in a group therapy session with a therapist who told me I could not write notes during 'group'. Jeff Schwartz, the administrator for the facility at the time, informed her that I had a hard time understanding things, and that notes helped me. She said I could leave group or stop taking notes. She was the only person in the group upset with my note taking. So I left, and got a razor out of the bedroom where I had hid it and cut myself to relieve the shame I felt for trying to help myself.

This therapist would always place me in the back of the van behind the seats because I was a guy and the girls needed to have seats. There are people – and therapists – who want to help others, but who cannot even help themselves. I do not blame this therapist for what she did. She was just being who she was, and she had issues with men that were not resolved and became a therapist to help women who suffered like her. I have met many therapists like her since that time, and it is sad, because they still harbor anger toward men and while treating men they are not able to really separate their anger.

The same facility had another psychologist test me. She came back with the results that my father had sexually abused me for many years. It was odd that she was so adamant about this, since I only saw my father three times in my life. She said that as a man I turned to food for relief because only gay men and men who have been sexually abused can have an eating disorder. The sad thing is she still treats people. I know before we help others we have to be sure we do not project our own issues on them.

I would like to see schools and parents get more education and awareness on eating disorders, obesity, and body image. I wonder, at times, what would have happened if my mom or I had information on eating disorders and body image issues while I was growing up. Today I deal with schools that do not discuss this, but which have kids who deal with these problems. What has to happen before people stop labeling boys and girls and just let them be children and care for them as equals?

During the times that I was sick and had no help, I was accused by police officers in Los Angeles, California, of being high on drugs after I was stopped for a traffic violation. I had to walk a straight line, count, and say the alphabet before they would even listen to me. I explained that I looked like hell because I had just binged and purged at home and was headed to get more food. All they did was laugh and let me go. They thought because I had bloodshot eyes and was very drowsy that it had to be drugs. No – it was just me trying to heal my pain the only way I knew how.

After all I have been through, I can say I am a man, and proud of everything I have been through. The obstacles I placed in my way and those others placed in my way did not stop me from recovery.

Chapter Seven: My Higher Power

I was raised Roman Catholic, and growing up in a family where faith was always important gave me a sense of pride. I was excited to know that there was a power higher than anyone here on Earth who loved me and wanted the best for me at all times. As a child, I was able to turn to my higher power, who I called 'God,' for guidance, love, help, and understanding. My mother and grandmother had great faith in God, and lived their lives working to help others better their lives. Mom and Grandma never put themselves first, because they thought it was selfish and not what God wanted for them.

Even though I was very grateful to have a higher power as a kid, I always thought it was very odd that we had to say confession in a box behind a curtain to the priest who already knew who I was. Did it make it easier for him to give me my penance? I don't know, because I would ask this and he and the nuns would tell me that this is what you do and not to question God. I was a kid and had many questions. I was not questioning God – just trying to find answers to everything. After he gave me my Hail Mary's and Our Fathers, he would tell me to ask for God's forgiveness for my sins. Hell, I was in grade school. What sins had I committed that I needed to ask forgiveness for? I was taught that you obey your parents and follow the Bible and, if you stray from that, it is a sin. It was not a healthy way to build confidence in the church.

I did not blame God, because these words came from men and women who were put here by God and who chose to teach his word and book. What I did know is that these women and men were not perfect just because they chose to become nuns and priests. They were no more special than I was, but they were adults so I listened – and questioned everything they had to say. I did not believe something unless there was a reason behind it.

Being taught that God knows everything we do confused me when it came to confession and church. If the Big Guy already knows, then why do we have to do all this ceremonial crap to get Him to love us? Father Casper, our Irish priest at Holy Cross, was a good man but flawed in many ways. He acted as if he were God at times, and struck fear in kids as often as he could so that we would grow up to be good Catholics – not good people, but good Catholics. What the hell was he thinking?

I knew early that you cannot scare a child or an adult into following God, because at some time she or he was going to rebel. I did exactly that, and it took many years for my trust in the church to come back. I never lost my trust in God, only those people who claimed to represent His word here on Earth. I was not always the best child in grade school, because of the living hell the teachers would allow the other kids to inflict upon me. And these teachers were, in their words, put here by God to help others. 'Help' my ass.

One time, Father Casper told me that the other kids were just being kids, and that I should not be a big baby because no one likes a crybaby. I complained to him because I was standing in line after lunch and one of the boys ran full speed and hit me in the face with a tetherball. He had done it on purpose and everyone laughed, but Father Casper said I should just let it be. Turn the other cheek. Hell, if it had been him hit would he have just let it be? Hell no. That kid's ass would be burning as if he were in hell.

This was a man who was a complete ass my whole time at school, with me and other kids. He was reared in Ireland (as he always reminded us) and brought the old ways of dealing with children here to the United States. The teachers would think nothing of hitting us in class for reasons only they knew. I had missed a math problem one day in the fourth grade and Sister Cathleen hit me over the knuckles with the sharp end of the ruler. I missed the rest of the problems that day to show her she was not going to get the best of me. Each time she hit me and the knuckles bled by the end of the class. Boy, it hurt like hell, but I would not give in then and I have never given in since.

My understanding of the Bible when I was growing up was that men wrote it. It needed a woman's input and still does, because there were great women then other than Mary the mother of Jesus. As man is imperfect, I have always believed that man's need for power, acceptance, and control influenced the Bible as we know it today. I am not saying that the Bible is wrong, or that it is not a great book. I am saying people need to question things more instead of just accepting what was written years ago. I accept some of the Bible as God's work. Other parts I do not see as the words of the God in whom I trust and believe.

It is always a great joy to hear people of other faiths discuss their beliefs in a higher power. I respect and admire religions that are compassionate and are constantly looking for the betterment of mankind through love and nurturing. Those that need to force others to believe as they do, in my opinion, doubt their faith and themselves. I doubt man, not

God. I believe that religion is man made and that spirituality is God given.

My spiritual side comes from knowing that everything I have done and that has been done to me had a purpose – a purpose more important than my own selfish needs and one I do not question anymore. I hated God at one time and thought that He did not exist. Why, if He loved me, would He let me suffer as I was or let me hurt others as I did. I always hear people saying that man has free will, and we choose to either be good or bad, and God only does good here on Earth. I respect that, but it is not how I feel. My God knows what we do before we do it. We are here to bring everyone together as a community someday. Everything good and bad has a purpose, and I know God allows us to suffer in order to see what we can do to bring suffering to an end. We choose to let our own needs overcome the needs of our communities, and that is not healthy.

I do know this: Being the type of person I was in my past, there would not have been a Saint Dennis who was God's right hand angel if I was alive back then and writing the bible. I am not perfect and nor will I ever be. I say this because I choose to believe that living a life of compassion is how we start to heal our own wounds and the wounds we inflict on each other. Do I want to be beaten, abused, shamed, ridiculed because I am different? Raped or even murdered? No. I do not want this to happen to me or anyone else, so I make the choice now *not* to do to others what I do *not* want done to me. It sounds easy, but it isn't. It has taken many years of questioning my faith to get to the point where I trust the higher power I believe in with all my heart and soul.

I know that Father Casper wanted people to feel guilty if they disobeyed what the church wanted them to do – as transmitted by Father Casper. Many people call this Catholic guilt; not me. I have no remorse for what I have done that was supposedly against being a good Catholic. I have broken some of the commandments more than one time. I have taken the Lord's name in vain. But I am working on that with the help of Dr. John Gardin, a great friend and confidant. I have not kept holy on the Sabbath day. I know damned well I did not honor my mother as I should have, and as for honoring Dad that was hard because he was not there. I never killed anyone. I am not sure about the adultery thing. Oh, yeah, I stole more than I ever needed. I bore false witness against my neighbor. No, my neighbors' wives did not do anything for me, but their goods always looked better in my house or my pocket.

I had my own commandments when it came to my eating disorder: "Thou shall not ask Dennis for food when he is eating." "Thou shall not ever say 'no' to Dennis." "Thou shall share what you earn with Dennis." "Thou shall not question anything Dennis has to say." "Thou shall honor Dennis because he has all the answers." I lived this way for many years. I actually believed that people should believe in whatever I said because my (distorted and dysfunctional) lifestyle was better than theirs.

I knew that, when I made the choices to have my own views on sex, abortion, marriage, sexuality, and family, the church would have different views and that people would cast me out as a sinner and heathen. The views we have are all shared by somebody someplace. When a religion condemns you for what you choose to believe, is it acting as the voice of God? I think it is not. Church leaders are wondering why people stray from their churches. It is because they have suffered enough abuse in their lives, and do not need to go to a place that is supposed to accept them and who they are, but instead chastises them if they have different beliefs or views on God and life. I know that religions tell people that if they do not abide by God's laws then they will not be loved as someone who does. Those of us who are strong in our own beliefs are then told we are not lovable, and we are shamed and cast away as sinners.

I did not want to live in fear of God for everything I did that someone else thought was wrong or immoral. I do not fear Him, because I am here because of Him, carrying whatever message He has chosen me to deliver in a different way from others. I am fine with that. He is my judge, not another man or woman on Earth.

When I was sick, I struggled with my belief in God and religion, but I know that no matter what tragedies I faced or trauma I went through that my higher power is what got me through day after day. When, as a child, I asked for help from all the abuse, the abuse kept coming. When I asked to have the pain in my head removed, the pain got louder. When I asked for acceptance from those around me, I was chastised even more. When I asked to die, I was left in more pain. I doubted God was there, but He was. Why did God let my Mom and Grandma suffer abuse at the hands of men? Why did He not let me have a father rather than just a sperm donor? Why did He take my sister-in-law away at such a young age? Why am I mentally ill? Why did He let those kids hurt me as a child?

You see, I asked for everything without ever doing anything to make the changes I had requested. I wanted God to just wave His magic wand and "presto!" all would be better. Once I was able to accept that I had to participate in what I did and be responsible for my part, I was able to see that the path that God chose for me had all these obstacles in it for a reason. I have never lost faith, but that which I doubted I have regained.

I talk with my higher power every day, and it is a great feeling not to be judged by my higher power for anything I say or do. The successes I have in life and those to come are not because I found God. No, I never lost Him and do not need to be born again. Once is enough, thank you.

My higher power gave me what I suffered through – my eating disorder, sex addiction, mental illness, pain, etc. – to share what I learned with other people and help them understand themselves. I am no better than anyone else, as I have said before. I am lucky in that I have had the chance to love myself again and accept who I am, not what others think I should be. I live life as it is for me today. Each day is a process, and I look forward to learning more and sharing with those who want to hear what I have to offer.

Chapter Eight: I Always Had Tomorrow

There will always be a tomorrow,
There will never be another today,
Don't let tomorrow be the answer
For what you choose not to finish today.

Dennis Henning, 2003

I can't believe it. Here we are again, sitting alone in your room with nothing to show for today. You still have no job, no apartment of your own, someone else is always paying, you are dirty, your clothes not washed, and you did not do a damned thing that could help us out of this hole you have kept us in all these years. This is why I am here. You need me. You have this fucking list and it is so great, according to you. What is so great about it? Oh, I see. If you did everything on this list you would have a productive day and feel better about yourself. I guess then all your problems would go away. Right.

That's real funny because this is the same list you have had for the last 19 years, and nothing ever gets done. And if, by chance or mistake, you do get something done, you have this great illusion that all is okay. Well, I can tell you why nothing gets done: You are a loser. A pathetic, fucking piece of shit who cannot do a damned thing for himself without fucking it up. Let's see: You sit every day in a café reading newspapers and books, hoping and praying to that God of yours someone will notice you and strike up a conversation. You want people to think you are an important person. You are not, never have been, and never will be. .

I can help you be important, but you keep running away from me. Even though you do have good intentions and are trying to do something, you cannot because you are lazy, immoral, ugly, fat, stupid, and worthless. Isn't that what all the kids used to say, even your friends? If everyone is saying it, it must be true. Even your dad did not want to be with you, and I am sure your mom would leave if she had a chance. The only thing keeping her around is your brother, not you. You are so fucked. But I will help you as I have always done over the years. You are afraid people will find out you are a liar, thief, manipulator, and have hurt everyone who has tried to take me away from you. I thank you for sticking up for me, but, damn, you are just not ever going to make it without me. Next to food I am your God, because we work to help you through all your tough times, then each night we talk to get ready for the next day.

Food is all you think about and sex is right behind it. Both are so good for you and soothe all the pain these assholes have brought to your life. I am glad we have food and sex to help us help you – God and I are tired of trying alone. From the time you wake up until you go to sleep, wherever that may be, you are thinking of food, what you can do to get it, where to get it, what you can do not to take time away from food. Food, food, food. It must be tiring. It is for me. Maybe once in this life you can do something without me to make it all better. I know you are trying and that is fine, but you can never be honest because then you have to tell the truth to yourself and people out there. You know the truth: Without me and what I give you each day, you are nothing. I give you food, sex, money, and the people who are so disgusting that they need some piece of shit like you in their lives. If any of this changed you would have to give up stuffing your face with food and stealing for the fun of it and the sex every day with someone new. Wow, you've got it made.

You like shitting your bed, throwing up on yourself, and lying there all night. You must like it – you do it all the time. You do nothing to stop it. By the way, I am sorry you make that damned list of things to do and then make those promises to yourself every day. You have so many notebooks filled with words and they are just words with no substance. Why do you do that? Why do you write all the time? It doesn't do you any good, you know that. I know that the list calms your nerves every night, giving you false hope. Are ya stupid? How about your promises to God every night to let the list come true? You asshole. You have to do things to make it happen, not just pray. Hell, even God is tired of your pathetic shit. He keeps you here just to see your ass suffer. He hates you more than you hate yourself. He told me so. Why does He hate you? Because you are a coward who does nothing each day to make your life better or to help others around you. Look, go ahead and look at yourself. You are a fucking loser. A mess. You are fat and ugly. Even your family does not want you around.

You cannot get a job because you are too lazy and afraid to be around people. No one will hire you because you are dumb and stupid. You have no education. Boy, are you sad. Those kids were right about you growing up. You know it and so do I. You are like a big baby who can't even wipe his own ass. Come on, you take 200 or 300 laxatives a day to lose weight because you want a quick fix. You are so lost in that little pea brain world you have made for yourself. You are afraid of every bite you take, but you eat all day long. What the fuck is that about?

Hey, why do you always tell everyone how great life is when you can't even get out of bed when you shit yourself? You want everyone to like you and to think you are doing something important. How pathetic is that? If you are not eating or stealing to eat, you are fucking some woman day and night. God, that is awesome, all the sex you want and no attachment. You are an empty shell, without any future. Nobody wants to be with someone like you and you know it. Come on, no job, no education, no future. All you do is eat, lie, steal, and fuck. Now those are great qualities – if you are in jail. Nobody wants you. Only I can stand your shit and I would leave this empty head if I could. But for some reason I am here and can go nowhere else.

Let's pretend we are having a perfect day. I have told you many times, although you never listen, that if we can visualize it, it can come true, and we can do it. I know you can do it and I believe you have the ability, so take a deep breath and quit crying, you fucking puss. You are always fucking crying. Your list for today was to take a bath, wash clothes, call for jobs, read, write, have only two meals, not spend over $20, see a movie, call your mother, pay bills, clean the apartment, and whatever else was on the list. Okay, now we are just sitting here in the corner rocking back and forth on the floor naked. What the hell is that about? Did you shit yourself again? Would you pul-leeze stop the goddamn fucking crying like a two-year-old? I am trying to help you and you are not listening to me. Hello, hello – anyone home in that thick fucking head of yours? "Listen up and stop the fucking crybaby act. I know *your head hurts because you slammed us against the wall, but we did not pass out this time. I am getting stronger, so whatever you do to get rid of me, it is not going to work. You know this cutting thing is never going to stop me from living here in your head. Sure, I'll go away for a while, but I come right back. I can never go away because you need me and I love you, man. Hell, no one loves you as much as I do. I make everything better, so cut the crap and stop trying to get rid of me, because you are the one that gets hurt, not me.*

Who is going to free you when you are in pain or find the women for sex or help you set someone up to cheat or steal from? Who? No one but me, baby, only me. Each time someone gives you a little more money to push them further during sex, who tells you it will be okay? I do. Who makes everything better? Me. Remember, you are nothing, because I make you who you are. Without me, you will die.

"So, we find a job, cook at home, stay with one woman, see family more, be honest to others, stop isolating so much, stop cheating and lying and manipulating, then do what we have to do. Think about it. What do we have? You are a freak of nature because you cannot control your eating and self-abuse, you so-called 'man'. Hell, you are a fucking sissy because you have a woman's disease. You fuck head. If you did do all these things you would become responsible and accountable for everything you do and say. That is too much for me to handle and you as well. You would have to grow up if you did not have me here to help you and love you each day no matter what you do. I know I am a little hard on you, but I am better than some stranger telling you what to do and

that you are wrong all the time. Can you see what life would be like without me? I am your best friend, your confidant, your Higher Power. If God really cared he would not let us suffer as we do. I care and I do the best to make your life better. Your identity is through me. No one would even look at you if I did not plan your day each day.

I make others like you. Remember that. We work together to trap others in our needy world to help us. You can't come up with all these ideas on how to make things happen, without me. You are not that smart. I allow you to be free. If you do start to finish things as you have tried, who will you turn to for help when things fall apart again, and they will? Why suffer the humiliation and defeat? Let's just stay here, where we are safe.

I make sure you never forget this. Why do I always have to remind you? Why? Okay, now we are calm. There is food in the fridge, by the bed, in your drawer, in the bathroom, under your bed, in the trash, and in the cupboard. Oh, yeah, if you want we can go see the strippers around the corner to just relax and have fun. It is up to you. The clubs are open and you know all the sex you want is there anytime we go out. Let's go get laid and fuck all night until tomorrow. Come on. Then we can just hang out here tomorrow because we will be tired. Another excuse to add to your pathetic life. Sorry, but we can do whatever you want. Hey, the computer is on. Let's search sites for real hardcore sex and other crazy things. Just a thought. You deserve this after the hell I just put you through. But, you have to understand I do it because I love you and I don't want anyone hurting you. I need a break. Just to go out and have fun. I will be here, waiting, as I always do. No, wait, wait. Damn, I almost forgot, sorry.

Remember tomorrow is a big day. We start all over again. Just because you sat in a café for four hours today, made up stories to people to cover up what you do not do, had sex this afternoon for money, blew off bill collectors, lied to family and friends, saw two movies, not just the one you planned, and spent $300 on food, does not mean you cannot have a productive day tomorrow. Things can change. Only you never will. We can conquer everything together, you and I. We always have tomorrow.

I lived this emotional roller coaster for over 20 years of my life. Every day, come rain or shine, I had this going on in my head, whether I was alone or with other people. The only way I could deal with it then was to numb the pain with food or sex or both at once. These two self-cures that I thought healed everything were just illusory. They allowed me to have false hope that I could actually be productive outside of my distorted world.

Every moment I spent writing my daily lists was a moment that I actually thought I was making progress on my own. I felt as if I was able to contribute to my life in a positive way, and by following through I could cure the hell I lived in. I do know that I had maybe four or five nights in those eighteen years that I went to bed really knowing and believing I could change my life around to be productive and responsible for myself, without relying on my addictions and dysfunctional lifestyle for the answers. But, it was so hard to ever get things going in a positive way because I always wanted things now, not yesterday or tomorrow, but right now. I did not want to take the time to change until I discovered that *The Daily Process, 16 Points to Life*© slowed me down to take the time and see that it is within my reach to accomplish anything and everything I want. But, I have to take it one day at a time and be accountable for what I do.

Every morning I was so excited to read the list and then get ready for the day. It was a new day in my world, but in the real world it was the same thing with the same outcome. I just did not want to believe it. In reality I could not change me because I did not know how and would not let others in to help me. It was my way or the highway, a cliché but the truth.

I wanted so much to show everyone that I was capable of making things happen for me and them, that I never realized that I had to do for me first, before I could do for others. I would always blame others as well, because I was trying to change for them and they could not see it. And if I changed, they would benefit from what I did. By allowing myself to stay with those around me who were as sick and dysfunctional as I was meant to stop really trying to change. I had no examples in my life, and the good examples were people who I would not let in, like my brother Richard, the only person I have ever admired. In my world we stuck together and fought those who tried to change us. What I did was to keep running until the day I realized I could not run any more and had nowhere else to run.

If you have seen the movie "Groundhog Day," with Bill Murray re-living the same day over and over and over, then you have seen what I mean by always having tomorrow. But, in that movie, he tried to get out of that cycle. In my life I kept going back, because it was the only thing I thought I could have. If I could not escape what I was, I would embrace it and endure.

On top of this crazed daily list, I had other rules that I had to abide by in order to feel good about anything. If I was looking for a job, I had to weigh a certain weight before I felt good enough to have someone see me – and then I knew the weight was the reason I got the job. If I felt I looked good, then everything else would be perfect. I had to have 72 hours without a binge/purge episode and eat three meals a day, and I would be cured.

I know now that what I did was allow myself to be seduced by the distorted belief that there will always be someone out there to help me if I was sick. Someone is always willing to work on us rather than themselves. So two dysfunctional people cause more trouble that cannot be overcome. At times, I wanted to get better. When I was at my rope's end, I took a risk and it worked. I was afraid that if I lost my daily habits and identity, I wouldn't know who I was or what I had left behind. I felt as if the voice in my head was right, because everything I had experienced up to that point in my life was emotional abuse and I knew no better, so I might as well do the same thing. I was scared to be me. I had to be someone else in life for anyone to love me or like me. I had to show everyone that I was important. Sadly, I was not important enough to myself to get help.

I realized that, in order to escape this treadmill, I had to look at what I did each day, find what set me up to fail, and make the changes that were needed.

I completely stopped writing lists in 1997, because writing lists set me up for failure in the past and I thought I could handle it. What I do now is work each day with the knowledge that I have tomorrow to finish what I need to finish. I do not have to abuse myself because I was unable to get things done. I am not perfect, nor have I ever been. I always thought I had to do everything perfectly to get any results that were worth anything. In *The Daily Process, 16 Points for Life*©, Point Number 12 says, "Tasks left undone from my list each day mean only that I now have the time to finish them when the time is right. I do not have to be angry or abusive to myself because I feel as if I have failed. I succeeded to the best of my ability today." This is how I live now and I know the triggers that can set me back. It is a choice – my choice.

Chapter Nine: *"I Did It My Way"*

I think we all have a character trait that dominates us at times even if we do not want to admit it. The trait of mine that always excited me and gave me a thrill was to be overpowering to everyone and everything that got in my way. I had to be on top of everything and it went my way no matter the outcome for others or me. When I say "my way," during my dysfunctional days I had no idea where I was really going, but I wanted no one to change the course I was pursuing. Because I knew, with outside influence, I would have to look at *me* and be responsible. Not something I was willing to do at that time.

By being the one thing I always told myself I would never be allowed to be (a helpless man), my distorted views, thoughts, ideas, and actions were validated. I took on the role of victim in my mind and never let it go. In my distorted world, I was justified in whatever I said, who I hurt, stealing, gambling with others' money and lives, cheating, lying, fighting, my sexual lifestyle, manipulation of others and their emotions. This included the destruction of my family, because I always felt that it was me against the world and that, if I did not strike first and lay down a foundation, others would do to me first what I had to do to them first in order for me to survive. It was survival of the fittest – with no rules. With no arms, I was fighting a heavyweight champ and I was winning. Impossible, except in my distorted world.

I knew that if I let someone get close to me I would be abandoned, shamed, or hurt. I also knew I would have to be honest about who and what I was as a person, and the other would see that I was weak. As a coward, I was a bully again, just like those who bullied, shamed, and degraded me – the ones I hated – when I was growing up. It is so true that we hate in others what we see in ourselves and that was true for me. Many times I felt like such a fraud, but I was so overboard in my ways that I could not bring myself back to reality – a reality that I now know is the foundation of my success. Today we choose to build foundations in our lives, and what we put into our foundation is either dysfunctional or healthy. My first foundation was built on fear and fear alone. Fear fueled my dysfunctional lifestyle.

My eating disorder became my primary ally when others attacked me for my lifestyle. It soothed my need to be liked and accepted by others. Even though I suffered in silence for many years, I would never let others see what I went through alone, or let them know my true feelings about me. I lived behind a façade, wanted the respect of others – because I had no self respect, I thought their respect would make it better – and would do anything to prove myself to them.

But I had no self-respect or love for myself or understanding of what could happen to me. I knew that with the life I led and the things I had done to others, only someone else could stop my suffering and self-abuse. I could not stop myself in the emotional state I was in. I felt someone would have to take my life in order to stop me or that I would end up in prison until my death, because I was a coward. I figured I was going to keep up my ways until one of those two things happened. I wanted and needed someone to stop the monster I was, because I could not do it alone. (I learned later in life that *I* was the only one who could stop *me*, 'the monster'.)

The day I conquered this monster, I was alone. I was humbled by the realization that my self-hatred was the monster and that I could love myself as others had. I saw what I had done to so many people and to myself. At that moment I knew I had a choice. Point Number 10 in *The Daily Process: 16 Points to Life*© says, "I have forgiven myself for what I appeared to be." I appeared to be a monster, when in reality I was a scared and lonely man, a broken man, no better than anyone else and no worse off in life.

If I wanted to stop hating myself and being a victim, I would have to do something that was even scarier than the lifestyle I led: I would have to change. I did not know if I wanted to or if I really could. In my mind, I had no justification to change anything in my world. What could or would be better than what I had? I did not know the answer, so it was easy to stay in my little dysfunctional world. I had no one to answer to because I set it up that way. I did not answer to my family, the law, rules, or God. I answered to whatever made my day easier to live through. Whatever I needed to get through the pain I took or went after. I had never looked at the outcome of my behavior before I did anything.

I would lie, steal, cheat, or manipulate, and then I would justify my actions because I was always right. In the real world, I was seldom right. I had no need to care about the outcome of my actions, because I lacked love and respect for myself. Nor did I worry if something would happen to me and to others at the same time. In my world other people were responsible for themselves, even if I could control what they said and did, because I knew my needs were the only needs that counted. It was a constant thrill for me to put things over on other people, because it was all such a game. I had to win that game at all costs, even if it meant sacrificing everybody and everything.

Living this way for over thirty years prevented me from getting many beautiful things that I wanted: A great relationship with my family, a girlfriend, friends, respect, travel to beautiful and far away places, an education, and a relationship with my higher power. I stopped myself from having any of it. My emotional issues blocked my every move because in my head those things were for other people, who were good. I hated myself for who I was and the things that went on in my head.

To this day, my brother Richard is the only person in my life I have ever admired. He has always been a strong pillar for everyone to lean on – family, friends, and especially me. For many years I pushed him away, because I was embarrassed and ashamed of myself and the life I led. Rich always has the right answers to things because he uses logic. In the past we would argue, and it was always easy for one of us to walk away. But we both hurt very much from these confrontations. Rich always wanted to know why I did not just get a job and pay my bills. We differed from each other in many ways. No one could tell me what to do or how to do it because I was the one who was right. How could I give up that feeling for a nine-to-five job? That couldn't happen.

I was not going to share my creative ideas with someone and not be rewarded. I had to find my niche, and it took me over thirty years to get here. I always had an answer for my brother's questions, but it was always a lie or an excuse, never the truth. I was scared to try to live a normal life like other people. I had all the answers, but no solutions. I learned later in life that everything I do is a process – positive results happen when I do the work. When I apply myself there is nothing that I – or anyone else – cannot do in life. I know this because each time I attempt something now, I have the courage to ask for help and let others share their ideas, thoughts, and opinions with me.

From 1980 until 1996, I would work really hard for a short period of time, stay busy and productive, but when things began to show promise I would hide in my dysfunctional world and everything would fall apart. This was a pattern and always reality for me. I was scared to leave my safe and unhealthy lifestyle, and would do everything possible to sabotage myself. I knew I could start all over again with this cycle and feel as if I was really making something happen each time. It was not because I could not make things happen, it was because I was afraid of what responsibility might come with the success.

During 1993, I had been living in Sacramento, California, getting money from my mom, brother, and odd jobs. My mom and I have always been the best of friends. She always stood by me no matter what I did. I knew I could get anything from her even if it meant her sacrificing what she needed at the time. I used her and lied to her on a daily basis without the blink of an eye.

Mom wanted to visit her cousin in northern California and asked me to go with her. I agreed. I didn't know any of my mom's father's side of the family and this would be the first time I met her cousin, Champ. We drove through this very small town, and I was bored and didn't want to be there. I noticed a bar and restaurant that were closed down. I asked Champ about the bar, and he told me about an old

German woman who owned the bar and the history it had in the town.

The owner was not liked or loved by the town folks I spoke with that day and the bar was for sale. I liked challenges, and this was one I knew I could win. The town had one little store, no traffic lights, and one gas station. It was small, but right off the I-5 freeway near Sacramento, California. The traffic and potential customers for a bar and restaurant were right there. I knew that I could get the bar up and running, and that I could do it with no money of my own – only my ability to create and manipulate.

In all the craziness I was about to create in my life and the lives of those around me, I did not really consider that my brother was still grieving from the passing of his wife, Carrie. He was going through so much, as was the entire family. He was trying to rear two little boys without their mother. Despite this, I decided to make this bar a reality. I had no money, but knew my brother would help once I got things rolling because he believed in me and I was good at manipulating him to help me. At this time I was so sick with my eating disorder that it was another way for me to live in my disease and no one could really see me. A new town, with new people who did not know anything about my illness or about me, sounded great.

I worked for three months to open the bar. I was there day and night, working and dealing with everything needed to make this happen. I had local businesses donate materials to redo the inside and my brother paid for the other things we needed. The owner gave me three months rent free so we could get everything ready to open. I made deals with liquor distributors on the booze and beer, and set everything in motion to make this happen. I knew if I kept busy I would be all right.

At night I would go to my brother's house to steal food from his kitchen – always making sure I took food from the back so no one could see that it was gone – and money from my little nephews' piggy banks in order to feed my pain at being afraid of life and the fact that I could not make the bar and restaurant happen in my state of mind. But I really thought I could make this happen and be successful at the same time. During the day I worked and at night after eating I would go to strip clubs to feed my sex addiction. I was lonely and these clubs were a place of serenity for me. As long as I was in the club, I was not going to eat or do other things that could hurt me. In my mind the clubs never were a problem. In reality I spent thousands of dollars for this so-called serenity. Some of the money I actually earned, but most was from stealing – from myself and others – or lying – to myself and others.

The town rallied behind me because I wanted to bring people to town to spend money at the bar and other businesses. The local newspaper ran an article on the bar and a section of the bar that had all the names of the townspeople who were killed in war. It was a great marketing tool and a way to bring attention to the bar. Later when I was unable to continue working the bar, everything that had been done and the money my brother and another investor put in was lost forever. My dream of making everything better ended up, as always, down the drain because I could not – and would not – get healthy.

My brother was convinced by my passion, and his fear that I would do something stupid to myself, like commit suicide, if this did not work out persuaded him to put money into the bar and secure the liquor license for me. He had what I never worked for: Stability, a job, and structure in his life. He ended up losing money in this venture, but he stood by me all the way. In my mind I understood what he was going through with the death of his wife and the reality that he was rearing two boys alone. But I needed help – and he was the one I pushed into putting what he had on the line to make my distorted needs come true.

He fell for my lies by believing that I was really going to change my life to make this happen. Two weeks after we opened, I hated being at the bar and so spiraled deeper into my addictions. I lived behind the bar in the back of the building. It became my little den of dysfunction. My room was a big studio with a bathroom and a bed, nothing else. It led into the kitchen and bar, so it was easy to go back and forth whenever I wanted. I used the room for sex and gambling every night, during work or after work. I brought in the local women I had been seeing, customers' biker babes, female bartenders, female truckers, any woman. The sex and food were the medicines that kept me going.

In the bar we had a dart machine and I played games for as much as $1,000 each. Soon I was hustling money from the people who came in to drink and have fun. I lost as much as I won, but it was fun. There was no one to answer to and no one to tell me what to do. I had a video game installed that I could switch from a normal game to a gambling machine. People would play that all night. I would make up to $300 a night off this machine. I ran everything and could cook the books and tap the machines with ease. No one knew I stole from myself to feed my habits. The genius in me.

After we opened, and after I became very distant from everything and did not want to be there, I used food and sex at a pace that I had never done before. I could not handle working there, so I had to make excuses to have people work for me. I had employees who were stealing from me and I did nothing about it, because I would have had to work and I did not want to do that.

I continued to let my brother think I was okay and that everything would be fine. We were losing money and it was because of me. It had to be my way, and, if I did not tell anyone, then it was okay. I would not admit the bar was failing, not matter what the cost to others or myself. My concern was for my well being, and at that time my well being was to feed my addiction, no matter what I had to do or how many lies I had to tell.

Leigh was a local woman, a bright and beautiful lady and a recent widow. She was the first person who I had met that I could speak with about all my problems. She knew nothing of my past and that felt great to me, someone to start over with as a friend and not be judged. She listened and cared, for whatever the reason. It was the closest I have ever been to a woman emotionally. She had three great children, and reminded me of my mom, raising the kids by herself. We played darts, gambled, and had fun together. She became very close to my mother and grandmother. It was so peaceful to watch her and my mom and grandma together, and the respect she showed them meant so much to me. I felt at peace when I was with her. The bar was losing money and I needed more to keep it open. I went to Leigh to offer her part of the bar as an investment.

I needed to give money back to my brother and to keep the bar afloat. Leigh invested in the bar and things turned around a little. I was really getting worse and could not function to even stay awake most of the day. I knew this when she invested, but I thought I could get better and make it all work. She knew I was sick and still believed in me. Needless to say, I failed. It got so bad that my brother had to clean up the mess. He and Leigh lost all the money they put into the bar.

I knew from day one that I was not able to stay with anything, but I wanted to try the bar – and it had to be done *my* way. Before I went into rehabilitation in July, 1994, I took all the money that was in the business account and went to Lake Tahoe, Nevada, to play one last hand of baccarat. I thought I could win back all the money I owed everyone and then everything would be okay. I drove for five hours from Sacramento, and stopped every place I could to eat and purge. I had big baggy pants on, long hair, a bandanna, earrings, big boots and an oversized jacket. I looked like shit and felt even worse, but, damn it, I was ready to change my life and all I needed was one big score, one last time. There was always one last time for me then.

My vision was so blurry from throwing up and not sleeping for three days that when I arrived at the casino they watched me very closely. I knew I could win, I just knew it. All would be fine. I walked up to the table and bet $15,000 for one hand. The dealer asked me if I was sure and the pit bosses came over to discuss something before they let me play. I was nervous, scared, sad, depressed, and had that high of knowing I could win. I only needed one win. I lost. I stood there for what seemed like eternity and as I was walking away the dealer gave me a $20 chip to get something to eat. I left the casino and went back to Sacramento, never telling anyone about the loss. The first thing I did was lie about where I had been and binge on food and sex at my little studio. I was having a sexual relationship with a biker and her girlfriend, so we ate and fucked and they drank for three straight days.

I had inflicted serious damage to the lives of my brother and Leigh and their children, by taking the money that was set aside for their future. I did not care about what they needed, because I had to do everything my way. I did not see – or want to admit to myself – that I was the cause of all the problems as they were happening. I played on the losses in their lives – their spouses – and knew they would help me. They thought they would gain by investing in me – not in the bar, but in me. I was never able to complete anything before opening this bar, because I always started things and then just walked away when work or responsibility got in the way of feeding my addictions. Nothing could keep me away from food, sex, gambling, and other compulsive behaviors. If something such as a job or commitment started to get in the way, I walked. So, I did what I always did: I walked away from the bar and left my brother and Leigh to deal with the mess.

I left town and moved to San Francisco, to try to deal with my eating disorder and be near my therapist, who really helped me. I ignored the tornado I created and knew my brother would clean up behind me as he always had. I thought I would find a job and get things going in a positive direction. Another town, another life to start over in my distorted little world. Do you see the cycle?

But as usual I was wrong. I could not start over because I never stopped living in my dysfunctional world. With a new apartment, town, clothes, etc., I was still the pathetic person I had always been. I still lived off other people's money and exploited their love and concern for me. Leigh helped pay for everything in San Francisco, and would come visit me. We always had fun. I told her and my family that I just needed to get better, and then I would be able to fix everything that I had destroyed. I was worse than a hurricane – you can see a hurricane coming, but I made sure no one saw me until I left. I still could not make any changes. I ran from one mess to create another mess. That was just the way I lived my life, leaving other people behind to clean up the lives that I had taken apart. I thought that they were adults and responsible for their own actions – if they wanted to be part of what I was doing, it was their fault as much as mine. But in reality, the blame was mine and that is the truth. I ruined others to feed my distorted world, and then blamed *them* if they got angry or upset.

I was happy in San Francisco, because no one could see me and I did not have to worry about dealing with my family. I sank deeper into depression and paranoia as time went by. I was still doing it my way and that was enough for me. In my grandiose world, I lived like some great leader who becomes power hungry and self-serving, who loses his vision. I did not know who I was or what I was. I had become a shell waiting for life to just happen without effort. My way of life almost killed me and always damaged the lives of others for over thirty years. This is what I knew and how I survived.

In July, 1994, I sat in my apartment in San Francisco stabbing myself with a small pocket knife and a fork, then pouring salt in the open wounds. I kept calling people I knew and rehabilitation centers, hoping that someone would reach out to help me. I was scared and knew that, if I was going to die that day, it would be because I always did what I did for me. I sat knowing in my mind that the payback for my lifestyle was to die in that room, all alone because I let no one else in my life and listened only to myself.

Once again, my family stepped in to help. My brother and mother sent me to a rehabilitation center in Southern California. I had hit bottom, and the people I used to get to the bottom were the ones who saved my life. I saw what I had become, and knew that I wanted to change. It was up to me. That day I made the first positive choice I had ever made in my life. In therapy I learned there were others like me, and that I could look at what I had done in my past to survive with clear vision, knowing that I could not change the past but that I could make my future better – and I have.

Chapter Ten: My Caretaker and Best Friend – Food

I sat alone in my apartment in San Francisco, looking at the numbers turn on my digital clock. It felt like an eternity between each number flip. I felt anxious and nervous. It was 8:30 pm and I waited for my food orders to arrive. I was nervous, embarrassed, and ashamed because I had ordered from two different places. I did not want the delivery guys to see each other and think I was a pig for ordering so much food. In reality, they never even cared about what I was doing or eating as long as I ordered food and paid. In my mind, I thought they would see me as a disgusting pig and make fun of me, then go back to work and talk more about me.

It was another day in a two-week period during which it was very hard for me to function in any capacity that would have been productive and beneficial in any way to me or to anyone else. The void in my life at this time was always filled by food. When I was awake and when I was sleeping, I dreamt of food. The dreams were so vivid and real that I would wake up feeling full and sick and soaking wet from the anxiety.

There were so many things I wanted to do, had planned to do, but was not able to do because I was frozen in time. I wanted to leave my apartment and look for work and do other important things that could help me, but I knew that I would not be able to deal with people or reality if I ventured out from my apartment. To overcome these anxieties, to numb the pain I experienced, I ate as often as I could. I never deprived myself of my daily medicine to cure my emotional pain, and my self-prescription was food.

I was so excited for night to come each day, because, if I got through the day without abusing food or myself, I would be on the road to recovery and on my way to curing myself from all the demons, pain, and voices in my head. It was all to no avail because, as usual, I couldn't make it.

The following morning, after a day and night of consuming over 25,000 calories, my fear was *so* strong. But I knew I had to go out and try to make the things I had on the list I made each day – look for job, go to gym, read, consume no trigger foods like candy, fried foods, pizza, cakes, etc. – become reality. As I dressed, I kept telling myself that I would just walk for a couple of blocks to a little café near my apartment and then start the day. If I could do this I would be fine. I left my apartment and headed to the stairs because it was good exercise to walk them whenever I could – in my mind I was burning calories from the binge the night before – and then I kept my head down and just walked out the door. As I stood in the middle of the sidewalk, I had to figure out which way to walk so that I could not run into many people, taking the path less traveled by others that day to have a great day – at least in my head and world.

I walked up Van Ness to a local bookstore and my bus stop. I have always felt calm in bookstores. It seems as if I can disappear into a book and no one is going to interrupt me or speak to me. Each step made me aware of everyone around me, and I knew in my mind they were looking at me and laughing at the fat and ugly guy with the big jacket, bandanna, and army boots. My clothes allowed me to feel comfortable and kept anyone from seeing my ugly body. I knew I made a mistake when I came to a stoplight and everyone crowded around me waiting for the light to turn. People got real close, and it was so scary for me that I began to panic. I needed to get away from them immediately. I walked across the street while cars were coming because I had no other place to go. I avoided cars but still felt panic-stricken that I could be stopped by a police officer for what I had done. I looked back and the light had not turned, so the people could not catch up with me and I felt a little relief.

I knew that no matter where I was or where I went that people on the bus, at the gym, a café, a restaurant, on the streets, and even in the doctor's office were talking about me. I just knew it. I hated being in public or in the open because I was so vulnerable to others. Every day it was hard to focus and concentrate on the simple tasks at hand, because all I wanted to do was eat from the time I woke up until I either passed out from binging or fell asleep.

As I boarded my bus, it started to fill up with people. I felt trapped and scared that people would touch me. I headed over to Haight Ashbury, to my favorite burrito place in the whole world. The burrito only cost $2.99 and came in a tomato tortilla with red rice, chopped succulent chicken, onions, light salsa. Topped with a BBQ sauce I brought from home, each bite was so soothing and it took me about an hour to eat it, so I could savor the taste and hide in my world. If I liked a certain food I would sometimes travel up to three hours just to eat a simple meal such as a burrito, salad, or chicken dinner. That day I was so excited because it was burrito day for me, and I had waited the night before during another binge for the day to come. I wanted to beat the rush hour, so that I could be first in line and then out of there before the burrito place filled up like the bus had filled.

I got up early and went to the gym at 4 a.m. to start my day. I knew I was having the burrito and it had tortillas and rice with chicken. It was a big burrito and I wanted to work out hard to make it okay to eat the burrito. I was frightened that the two hundred laxatives I took the night before had not emptied my body of the all the food I had eaten, and so I needed to work out real bad. I was so tired, but I was not going to miss this workout. I did one hour on the treadmill, and with every step I felt like throwing up. My body hurt so bad, but I never stopped. With every breath and movement I felt the fat move on my body. I felt so ashamed, disgusting, and defeated. I continued. I followed this with one hour of weights and an abdominal workout. The entire time I felt fat and ugly and knew I was punishing myself for having no control over the amount of food I ate the day before. But, I thought, it was a new day and I could start all over. If I could just get through today, I would be fine.

My day was all set to start now and I was on my way. I had to be home by 7:30 a.m., and once there I had ten minutes to shower and change in order to be at my morning café to read my New York Times, San Francisco Chronicle, Los Angeles Times, and any other papers I could find, so I did not waste any time before the bus took me to lunch.

My bus ride was usually forty minutes and I had to walk eight long blocks that took twenty minutes more, so I had to leave the café by 9:40 to get to the bus on time. After I ordered my tea with honey at the café I began to read my newspapers. I was very crazed at this time in my life when I read. If I missed a word or read it wrong I would start all over at the beginning of the article. This made me pay close attention and I really concentrated hard. This was very time consuming, but it was the only way I could read. It felt productive to read, as though I was accomplishing something. I was invisible to everyone around me. I knew that no one would see me or hurt me if I just kept reading. It worked. Not only was I invisible to others in my mind, but I also used this time to hide from my responsibilities. I was so busy reading that I could not possibly look for work or do the things that could have made my day productive. I had to have a perfect day in order for a productive day to happen. I never had a perfect day.

I rushed from the café to the bus stop and had 20 minutes to spare before the burrito shop opened. This was going to be a great day; everything had been perfect so far. As I sat on the bus people began to touch me and push their way to seats. I got more nervous with every passing moment. I did not want them to feel the fat and ugly body I had to live with. I was embarrassed and afraid that they would laugh at me and belittle me. I sat there frozen, afraid to move or be seen. I thought if I did not move I would not be noticed. I wanted to ask for help or get off the bus, but I couldn't move. I was sweating as if I was on the treadmill at the gym.

While encapsulated in this fear and anxiety, I was not able to get off at my stop (not for the first time) and sat on the bus for three hours, riding around the streets of San Francisco. My mind told me to move, but I couldn't. If I moved people would notice me and laugh or make fun of the big ugly overweight guy, me. After what seemed an eternity, I got off the bus at about 2 p.m. I was so scared that maybe someone else besides the driver had seen me sitting there that I sat on the bench looking as if I was waiting for another bus. I even went so far as to keep looking down the street as if I was impatient. I was so upset because I had thrown off my perfectly planned day. All I wanted at that moment was a burrito, so I hailed a taxi and took a $12 ride to get a $2.99 burrito. I was so mad at myself that I decided to punish myself and walk home from the burrito shop.

I had no laxatives with me to take after my meal, so the walk would help me burn off the food. The walk took three and a half hours, and I was tired, ashamed, angry, sad, mad, vengeful, and demoralized. I just wanted to lie down in a garbage area to rest. I was so defeated. I knew I was a piece of shit for what had happened on the bus, and that I deserved to be with the shit and garbage on the street in some alley. I was so worthless at that moment that all I wanted to do was die.

During the day, I had consumed only the burrito, and the anxiety to find something to eat was making my heart pound so hard I thought it would come out of my chest. I dared not eat anything on the walk, because I feared that if someone were to see me they would think I was a pig or disgusting for having a candy bar or soda. As I walked home I felt everyone's eyes just seeing right through me. I knew if I stopped I would not be able to move again, because I was so scared and anxious. As I turned the corner and had my building my view, I picked up the pace as a race walker would. I got to my building and ran up the stairs because the elevator would have taken too much time. Once inside I locked all my locks and just melted into the floor and cried. I rolled up like a baby in a womb feeling safe and okay.

I quickly remembered that my curtain was open, slowly crawled over to the window making sure that no one could see me, and stood next to the window to see if anyone had followed me. I was frightened that someone might have seen the crazy fool I was during the day and followed me. I never really saw anyone following me, but it was routine to look.

I sat down in my favorite corner so that I could see the door and the window, in case someone was going to come in. I slowly began to rock back and forth, and cried silently at the humiliation I had caused myself this day for not being able to carry out anything I had planned. In between the silent tears I had bursts of anger toward myself. Here I sat, again, because I was not capable of doing anything that would be helpful to myself in my life. I was a loser with no future. I banged my head gently against the wall, then harder and harder until I was dizzy. Once I stopped hitting my head I began to pound my face, arms, legs, and stomach with my fist. I knew where the physical pain came from but not the emotional pain. If I could feel the pain I knew was okay, then the pain I had no control over – in my head – would go away. This is what I thought for many years. In reality, it never worked out that way.

Suddenly I stopped the self abuse, because I remembered that my twenty-four hour rule would be up at midnight and I had to eat everything I could by 11:59 so that tomorrow could be the day I was going to cure myself from all my food issues and eating problems. In my head, if I went for one twenty-four hour period on the schedule I had set for that particular day, I was okay. I would have made it through twenty-four hours and that is what I needed, in my mind, to be cured from all the issues I had, to prove I could do it alone. It was pure fantasy; I had a great imagination. To make sure I was on track, I always called the time on the telephone and stayed on until it hit 11:59 and the new day was here.

For the next twenty-four hours I was going to eat two small meals, work out in the gym, no sodas, no fried food, no candy, look for a job, follow through on everything I had not done the day before, drink only water, fruit for snacks, and nothing but water after 7 p.m. This was the best thing for me and each time I could not do this I started over the next day. The chapter on tomorrow tells it all. I destroyed myself each day for over eighteen years with this damned rule. It was so sad that I would do this to myself, knowing deep down inside I could never have this perfect day and if by chance I did, I was guaranteed to screw it up real soon. I knew that, when I did not make it, I had tomorrow to look forward to, to prove to myself I could do this. I was so preoccupied with this dysfunctional behavior and thinking that nothing else mattered.

I was so excited to have food delivered this evening because it would take away all the shame and guilt I had from this pathetic attempt to have a perfect day. I wanted the pain and humiliation to go away, and food was my answer. Whenever I ate at times like this, it was a ritual to set up everything so that I could eat without having to stop once I began. The first bite set in motion my descent into a euphoric state of mind that was second to nothing else I had ever experienced in my life. My sexual encounters were a close second. Everything and everyone around me slowed down when I went into this state of mind. It was slow motion at its finest. I liked this slow motion feeling because it seemed like it would never end. All emotional and physical pain I had felt at that moment or during the day was gone with the first bite.

It was like an anesthetic, but, oh, so much better. I knew that my anesthetics in life were food first and then sex. If I could have both together all the time – and at times I did – the world could not have been a better place to live. Food became my caretaker in life. My attachment to food provided safety in my life and was what I used to respond to life. It became my identity.

After the day I had, I knew my compensation would be food and a lot of it. I ordered three large pizzas with ranch dressing to dip them in and a six-pack of soda from the pizza parlor around the corner. I always ordered from places close by so the food would get to me quickly. If it did not come in a time frame I thought was good, I would call until it was at my door. I also ordered fried rice, chicken chow mein, fried prawns, sweet and sour spare ribs, and steamed veggies from a Chinese restaurant. The total cost was $50 that night, and that was okay because I knew I would never spend this much again because tomorrow I would make the twenty-four hour rule work for me. At this time in my life I had brought my daily food bill down from $300 a day to around $200 a day. Progress is what I called it.

I was so excited to get the food and scared at the same time. Scared that I would not get it in the time I wanted it and that I could not eat it all before my 11:59 deadline. There was no way to avoid stress because I created so much of it. I wanted to shower this night to feel clean and relaxed, but I was afraid to see myself nude and touch my body. So I stayed on the floor staring at the door and waiting for the telephone to ring so I could let the delivery people up. When I found a place to order from I always said the food was for two or more because it helped with the embarrassment I would feel if they thought it was all for me.

As I sat there the buzzer rang, and it was the pizza man. I quickly buzzed him in and he came to my door. Because I did not want people to see me, I had a doggy door put in so that the food would be put through the opening. No one said anything about the doggy door because I kept to myself. As soon as I buzzed him in, I put on my tape in the next room that sounded as if I had company. This would give the delivery people the illusion that I was not alone and all the food was for a party or group, not one lonely depressed man who was so scared of people that he put a doggy door in. This deliveryman knew the drill and put the food in the door after I paid him. I always tipped real well, so no delivery person complained about my weird habit. I was craving the pizza and I knew the Chinese food could be warmed up, but pizza always tasted better real hot to me, so I did not have to see the grease from the cheese on the pizza after it sat for awhile.

As I sat down to eat the pizza the Chinese food arrived, so I buzzed the deliveryman up and did the same thing with the door and the tapes. In order to feel better about the amount of food I would order at restaurants, I took my nephews Andrew and Bo Henning, the two most precious things in the world to me, with me to eat when they came to visit. We went to the Hard Rock Café next to my apartment and we had a great time. Whenever I wanted to order takeout, I just ordered for the three of us and told the people there my nephews were with me again. I was ashamed to lie, but it was better than telling the pathetic truth. I did anything I could not to have others see me as a freak of nature for the habits I had about food and the large amounts I would eat.

I put all my food in the right places so I could eat it in sequential order before 11:59. I set up my food so that it was easy for me to get to when I sat down. I always wanted the food to be in an area the size of a small coffee table as if it were the face of a clock, so I could reach everything without really having to move. I didn't want to feel the fat on my body jiggle, and if I did not move much I did not feel myself being full or out of breath. I proceeded to place my pizza at 2 o'clock with the ranch dressing to dip it in. I placed the Chinese food at 8 and 11 o'clock with a towel over the boxes because I wanted to keep the food warm. After I placed the towel, I took the soda and put it in a line outside the clock area right next to the pizza. I had a cup of ice at 12 o'clock and kept refilling it after each soda. I wanted three sodas for the pizza and three sodas for the Chinese food.

I was all set now to violently stuff my face in the short time I had, so I did not violate my 11:59 deadline. I knew, if I did it before the time I had set, that tomorrow would be a perfect day and I could start all over with everything I needed to do to cure myself from the emotional pain I endured. I began to eat the pizza and with every bite I felt a sense of relief from the horrible and humiliating day I had just had. Each bite sent a warm and nurturing feeling to my brain and body, and I felt all the anxiety and emotional pain slowly drift away. My endorphins where flowing by this time. After completing two pizzas I knew I was full, but I told myself that the soda carbonation is what made me feel full. I waited a few minutes and ate the last pizza so fast that I bit my thumb and drew blood. This did not faze me or stop me. I wiped the blood on my shirt and continued to eat as the blood mixed with my pizza and dressing. Nothing was going to stop me from finishing what to me was the last binge of my life.

After the pizza and three sodas I went to the bathroom and took 80 laxatives. I was feeling so bloated, fat, ugly, and disgusted with myself at this time. But I had to finish the Chinese food or I was not going to make the deadline. I waited ten minutes and nothing happened in the bathroom so I went to the table and brought all the Chinese food into the bathroom and lined it up on the edge of the bathtub. I went into the kitchen and got more ice for the soda and returned to the bathroom. By the time I got there the laxatives began to work as they always did, and I lost control of my bowels and messed myself in my sweatpants. I did not skip a beat because this was something that had happened before. I quickly took the pants off and filled the tub with water and laundry detergent. I did not move any of the food on the ledge and sat down on the toilet. As I sat there I felt excited because I could eat my Chinese food and the laxatives would help it go right through me and I was going to beat the 11:59 deadline.

I had already envisioned the next day as the day I would cure myself from all my pain. It was now 11:30 and I had been in the bathroom for over an hour. I consumed all the food I had ordered and felt a sudden rush of anxiety. I was so tired from the long day and the binging and purging that I sat on the floor in the bathroom trying to figure out how I could get more food in the next twenty minutes. I had twenty minutes before my deadline, so why should I waste it? I could eat a lot of food, but I had no time to get anything else. I sat there looking at the empty containers in the bathroom and on the coffee table. I had only a tee shirt on and the floor was very cold. I was frustrated that I did not have more time to get some candy or something, but I calmed down quickly. I sat on the floor completely exhausted, defeated, head hurting, stomach bloated, with my throat in pain, and my ass on fire. I watched the digital clock next to my bed, adding minute after minute until it reached midnight. Those few minutes seemed like an eternity to me. But I had done it. I ate everything before the deadline and now, as I sat there, I planned the next day of my distorted life in my distorted world. Too tired to move and get into my bed, I pulled the towels off the rack to make a bed for myself on the floor. The smell coming from the tub bothered me as I lay there until 2:30 a.m., planning tomorrow and knowing it was going to start with the gym at 4 a.m.

This was a daily routine I never really knew how to stop or alter. It made all the pain go away, but it was a habit that had no redeeming qualities to it at all. I was lost with this lifestyle or without it. I kept it up because I knew that the pain of trying to stop was far worse than the anger, shame, guilt, and fear I faced every night after I started taking my medicine – food.

I knew other people did not live like this. Each time I was with someone who would leave food on their plate or have just a bite of candy or cake, my skin would crawl. How could they do this? It drove me nuts to leave one bite on my plate and to have one bite of cake or candy. If I could not eat it all, I was a failure or would not eat any. I realized in recovering that other people don't use food as medicine. There are people who can just eat when hungry and walk away. They can have a bite of candy or cake and be fine. They had healthy eating behaviors while I did not.

My days continued like this, blending with one another to the point I could not tell what day it was. They were all the same. I spiraled harder and faster each day into my dark abyss and the only ray of hope was food. It was my savior and devil wrapped together. I became an expert on choosing foods that would calm my anger, fear, anxieties, paranoia, sexual appetite, frustration, and self-abuse. The food did not choose me; I made it my medicine. I had a medication for every situation. The food made that moment so tranquil and peaceful that I kept returning to it no matter what it took to get there. The trigger foods I used at one point became anything that went into my mouth. I did not care; all food cured me. I could eat carbohydrates, fried foods, fatty foods, sweets, or even salads, grilled chicken, or vegetables. Large portions of one food could equal the numbing high I got from others. Where I obtained the food never mattered to me as long as I could have my fix. I got it from restaurants, trash bins, stores, garbage bags, or dog food dishes. I got it no matter what. The more I tried to make sense of this lifestyle, the more I ate and ate because I had no model to look to for help. I did not know that this was not normal. It was the life I had to live for all the bad things I had done. My pain was real and stronger than I was. I needed a fix and I never let that feeling down. There were several voices living in my head during these days and the conversations would drive me to eat even more. My eating disorder person, my self-hate coach, my maniacal exercise coach, my fucked up life coach, my sexually out of control person – hell, it was an orgy of one.

In 1993 I learned how much food really controlled me. I had been on a sex binge with over 30 women in a two-week period. I met these women at dance clubs, bars, restaurants, walking down the street, the gym, and even at church. During this time I would eat all day and have sex all night. Sometimes we did both at the same time and it was crazy and messy but, oh, so much fun. I started eating at 6 a.m. and stopped gorging myself at 5 p.m. I needed enough time to get rid of the food before I met my potential playmates. I would then go to dinner and the marathons of sex would take place. One day I had been to the gym to make room in my body for the large amount of food I was to consume that day. I ate so much that day I was scared to go to dinner that night with the woman I had met a week before, after I had had sex with her roommate. The night I had sex with her roommate she was going to join us but was scared because her roommate was bi-sexual and she had never been with another woman. So, we just made plans to see each other when we had the time. We discussed the three-way and left it open for her to explore if she wanted to at a later date.

We spoke at 3 p.m. and she had picked an Italian restaurant for dinner. Since I was so filled with anxiety I knew I could not just eat a normal meal that night. So I did what I knew would make my night easier and more relaxing. I informed her when we met that I was a little under the weather, but still wanted to have dinner with her and spend the night together. I let her know that I had thrown up earlier and that I may have to excuse myself to go to the restroom at any time. She was very sympathetic to this. What she did not know and what I would never have told anyone was that I visited the restaurant earlier in the day and placed food in heavy plastic bags with extra strong tape under the toilets and sink. I put several candy bars, cupcakes, candies and four boxes of laxatives in four plastic bags. I did not care if anyone found them because no one could trace them back to me.

At dinner I ate a four-ounce chicken breast with two small red potatoes and half a green salad with dressing. I excused myself to go to the restroom for a total of over 30 minutes in three separate visits. I knew this because she had timed me and was concerned if I needed to go home and rest. She was a very pleasant and caring woman. She was very comfortable with me and I with her. We talked about everything and anything, thinking we were changing the world with our very distorted minds. She did not know that when I went to the bathroom I literally had to clean crap and piss off of two plastic bags in order to get to my food. I did not care. Nothing was going to stop me from taking my medicine that night. I was very relaxed and calm by the time we went back to her apartment. We spent the night having great sex until dawn. Her roommate joined us the following evening.

Everything I did was planned so food could be my number one priority. If I needed a fix it had to be there. I have spent over half my life feeding my habit. I saw how crazy I had become and the lengths to which I would go to get my need met. I was out of control and scared. I thought about help, but it was not time. I could not stop.

As I became acquainted with the local restaurants it was always easier for me to go back. No one knew what I was going through, and it was easy to hide. I tipped very well and was a lot of fun to be around. I liked these places, not just for the food and comfort, but also for the bathrooms and the way I looked in the mirrors. I looked at my face, abs, arms, and sometimes neck to see if I gained weight before and after each meal. I felt thin because the mirrors at these places helped me look that way. Even if I liked the food and staff at a place, if the mirrors and lighting did not flatter me I would never go back. Food. It took care of me and was my only friend.

Chapter Eleven: Relationships and Intimacy

"I can't go out tonight because Rachel got home this morning and I have not seen her in two days," is what I heard from Mike on the other end of the telephone. I had called and planned to go out clubbing and dancing that night with Mike. But he was really set to see his girlfriend. She had only been away two days, but they had a bond that was special and agreed never to spend more than 72 hours apart. As much as one could tell from my point of view they had this great relationship they always talked about in almost a bragging way. When the three of us were together I would watch as they laughed with each other, complemented each other in many ways, held hands, kissed in public, and with small gestures showed affection that was tender and loving toward one another. Each time I witnessed this interaction and behavior it was hard to be around them. Not because they did anything wrong or that it seemed too much, but because I had never had this with someone. I felt sad and thought that I might never have this kind of relationship with a woman. It was something I always loved about other couples and wanted for myself.

Love is a hard word to understand or know. I hated myself, so why would any woman want to deal with the baggage I carried? To this day I get a wonderful and warm feeling when I see people being affectionate to each other (either physically or verbally), for any reason.

Since I dealt with so much ridicule and shame growing up, I was afraid that if I ever fell in love with someone and shared my past indiscretions, emotional illness and disease,

I would be shamed or judged for who I was. One constant in my life was my family's opinion. My mother and brother always encouraged me to build my relationships and settle down with someone so I would be happy and loved by that special person. What they did not know was that in each relationship the dysfunction was large and in charge. I never allowed my family to know much about my relationships because I did not want them to feel anything negative toward the women with whom I had relationships, good old people pleaser that I was.

After the relationships ended I shared with my family some of the hell that I helped create. No one person was to blame for the faltering relationships. I chose dysfunctional women and they chose me. It was true that I picked women like me in many ways, women who were insecure, afraid of love, lonely, needy, and had low self-worth. What my family did not know was how severe my eating disorder, depression, and sex addiction had become.

While growing up I had no positive examples of healthy and nurturing relationships between a man and a woman. There is no one to blame for that. It did not affect me then. I knew growing up that what we see on the outside does not always reflect the truth. I had so many people around me from neighbors to relatives and friends display love and affection in public, and then at home I saw the abuse and dysfunction.

It was very confusing and painful to see. My mom, grandma, and great-grandma raised my brother and me to be compassionate and loving to everyone, no matter who they were. Even with this instilled in me as a child I went on to abuse and victimize my family when I became an adult.

The strongest fear I faced every day until 1996 was the abandonment issue I had concerning my father and how he could walk away from two innocent children. I had no trust in people because I did not trust myself to open up and love or be loved. During this time of searching for love and acceptance with every woman I met, I knew my behaviors and actions in relationships and toward intimacy were distorted because food and sex ruled my life. I could not love someone else as I knew I wanted to love someone, because I had no love or respect for myself. I hated myself, and knew that in order for someone else to really love me I had to love me first. I could not bring myself to do whatever it took to love myself. I stayed in my distorted world because it was safe and warm.

Until 1996, ninety percent of my encounters with women were due to pure sexual attraction. Rather than getting to know each other or even our names, it was sex first and then whatever happened, happened. As I have said, my dysfunction brought more of those like me into my life. Sex was our motivation. I had more sex out of loneliness than any other reason. Whoever I was with wanted and needed the same thing at that moment, no matter the consequences. It was sex and nothing else. One moment of pleasure for a lifetime of hell.

My experience in monogamous relationships is limited. In my short and disturbed life I have lived with two women who were as dysfunctional as I was, but in other ways. I had one healthy relationship that ended because, if you can believe this, I would not take it to another level sexually. I was stunned and also felt proud of myself in this last relationship. It was the only healthy relationship I had ever had with a strong, beautiful, and healthy woman. I learned that sex was not the answer to everything and I did not want to hurt my chances with her by having sex too soon. At the time it ended she gave me an ultimatum to either have sexual intercourse with her or it was over. I declined because at that time it would not have meant as much for me as if we had waited longer. But, it was special. I knew with this woman I could love for more than just sex as the reward.

Living with the first two women made me see what I wanted and did not want in a relationship. They also showed me what I had to work on to make a relationship work. Cindy and Carla were as opposite as people could be. Both women were loving and nurturing, great cooks who had not dealt with their own issues in life. So together we fit our needs to a 'T'. Neither one had a healthy relationship with her father when we were together. Both loved me and I them the best we could. In truth, we should have never been together.

Cindy and I met on a Friday night in a Venice, California, nightclub called "Pinks." It was her thirtieth birthday that night and she was out to just dance and go home, nothing more. As I danced alone, as I did very often, I noticed her for over two hours dancing in the corner. I did not know if she was with someone and I did not care. I waited until it was near closing time and started dancing near her and we would dance together then drift off, but always watching each other. It was 1 a.m. and we had another 45 minutes to dance before the club closed. We moved slowly toward each other and in seconds we were grinding, sweating, and caressing each other through our clothes as if we were alone. We had no concern or worry about the other two hundred or so people who may have seen us. It was our world and others were just renting space.

There were no questions or names exchanged, we just worked ourselves into a sexual frenzy knowing that it was not going to stop there. I found myself following her through Santa Monica, Brentwood, and Bel Air, California. She lived in a guest house on a large estate in a little house that could have been taken from a fairy tale. As we approached the gate she drove in and I just made it before the gate hit my car. As we parked our cars and headed for the house I grabbed her and we had sex in her driveway under the light from the main house knowing that the owners could possibly see us. We did not care – it added to the excitement. Everything went so fast and one thing led to another and it was Sunday evening. We had not left her house for two days. The best part was we liked the fact that we did not know each other's names. It added to the sexual atmosphere and games we played with each other's body for two days.

That Monday morning Cindy had to go to work. When she left I stayed in bed and we looked at each other and knew this was going to be a roller coaster ride, although where it was going we did not know or care. We had a sexual appetite that fed us as one. That weekend was the groundwork for a year of sexual and emotional dysfunction.

Our passion for sex stopped us from seeing that we only hurt each other more, emotionally and sexually. As I had done with many other women, I misread sex for love and thought she cared. This time I was just with one woman and it made for an emotional abyss. There was no emotional connection between us from day one. Our whole lives together revolved around sex. We would eat then have sex. Argue then have sex. The louder the argument and the more angry we became, the better the orgasm for each of us. Straight lovemaking never happened. We did not know how to love, let alone make love. We did love each other in a very odd way. We were needy and kept each other from being alone. We pushed the boundaries of sex so far that we could not separate ourselves to see how bad this relationship had become. No one had satisfied our sexual needs as we did for each other and that was the fact. We did not communicate unless sex was part of it.

The relationship became violent at times for me. Cindy was 5'10" and a solid 135 pounds. She worked out, due to her own severe body image issues, and was very strong. She did not really have any skills at talking out differences and at times would become violent toward me. Since I was stronger I would hold her until she stopped and calmed down for a short period of time. At times she would punch me or throw things at me if I did not respond to her comments.

One Thanksgiving we were at a store getting items to have what I thought would be a nice peaceful dinner. As we were discussing the candied yams and sweet potatoes, I told her I wanted a sweet potato and put it in the cart. For some reason, when we got in line she told me I was not having the potato and I was going to have the yams. I said no and she went berserk. She went to the veggie aisle and threw everything in the bins while yelling at me. Once this was over, we went to my truck and she continued screaming and started to hit me in the face and upper body with her fist. It stopped once I informed her that one more punch would lead to an early exit out the door. When I got home, I called my brother and headed to Sacramento that afternoon.

She would get violent if I did not get jealous when she flirted with other men. I told her if she was going to have sex with someone at least to take a shower before coming to bed with me. She hated that I would not say anything to other men. But, I told her, "If you allow them to think you are single they will act as they do toward you." She loved and needed the attention no matter who returned it.

In this dark and dysfunctional world we created with each other, we were two lonely and sad people who had no self-love. We thought we could get it from each other; we were wrong. We had nothing in common other than sex. I liked to go out, she liked to stay in. I did not like parties, she liked parties.

Cindy was an amazing chef. She didn't know the severity of my eating disorder and would cook the most intimate and wonderful dinners. It was a production for her to cook and I helped by shopping and doing prep work. Most of the meals included a sexual experience that made both food and sex more exciting and passionate. Our sexual appetite for one another has never been matched, even in my acting out period of sexual addiction. Cindy knew of my sexual addiction and it was icing on the cake for us. We were two sex addicts living out that dream of sexual desires without boundaries or limits.

Cindy always thought I had a great appetite and just adored her cooking, which I did. But, my food addiction loved every moment of her meals. I knew in my heart, as she did, that once we took this relationship further it would not be healthy and the road would be a nightmare. But we both thought we could really be something special to each other. Our distorted reality did not allow us to see we had to love ourselves first in order to love each other.

Cindy and I would sit up until the early hours in the morning crying, laughing, and arguing about our relationship. We did not know any healthy relationships, so it was hard to compare ourselves to any. Sex was the glue, the equalizer for us. Our relationship was chaos, co-dependent with no growth. The sad thing is that we were great at this – blind to reality, because reality meant we had to look at ourselves, and we did not want to.

She was a wonderful and lonely person, looking for love but in the wrong way and from the wrong people all her life. I understood this and wanted to rescue her from her past pain. I thank God for the time we spent together because it has been a tool for me to learn. I learned that I needed to give to me first before I could give to a woman what she needs and wants. I had no idea what I wanted.

The old saying about wanting to have your cake and eating it too applied to Cindy. While we lived together I maintained contact to some degree with individuals who paid for my sexual services. This was fun but very challenging. Never once did I turn to them for money, even though it would have been easy. I knew once I did this any chance of anything positive with Cindy would be over. I know this contact was a barrier in my life from really connecting and sharing with anyone else. I had always known that sex was a powerful tool and I knew how to use it to get what I wanted. The power we experienced in our lives from our sexual strengths worked for us very well. We both wanted control and sex is what we used to gain and maintain it.

In my mind I had all these great fantasies of what it would be like when I met that one true love. It would be a partnership to share emotions, spirituality, needs and wants, desires and intimacy. It would allow respect, honesty, acceptance, passion, and trust to lead the way by honoring each other for who we are and what we are. I would hear what she had to say, as she would hear me, being a partner but an individual as well. These are the things I have yet to experience, yet need and want in my life. I know in order for them to happen, I have to have a solid foundation to build on. That is something I have now.

Frequently, in the past, I was in the wrong when I just walked away from people rather than accepting my responsibilities for my actions and behaviors. I always believed that since others were adults and everything was consensual, meaning we discussed how we felt about our relationships and life, whatever happened was meant to be. I was a coward because I let my fears control me and cowardice became my pattern with women.

I truly believe that anything worth having in life is worth 'dying' for now. I do not mean 'dying' as in six feet under, but 'dying' in the sense that it is worth the pain of overcoming my fears and putting myself out there for others to see the real me that I now know, love, and respect. By allowing this in my life now, I grow with each new experience I have with others. I *decide* if it is worthwhile for me to be involved. I do not walk or run away any more. 'Dying' is like a snake shedding – the skin has a purpose and then it is time to let go and rejuvenate with new skin. In my case it is a new look at myself with honesty and openness to accept others' intentions toward me without fear or resistance. There will always be healthy fear and that is good. It only becomes negative fear when I let it control me rather than confronting and working through it.

After my relationship with Cindy ended I went back to what I know best – hiding in sex without feelings or care. I found those who were like me, so there were no false expectations on either side. But then I met this amazingly beautiful woman, both on the outside and inside, who made me want to try and build a life with her. This time sex only played a part in the beginning. It was not the main factor as it had been with Cindy.

I had attended Alcoholics Anonymous meetings because I personally believe that the recovery in these meetings is stronger than those who attend Overeaters Anonymous. OA is a great organization, but I wanted to hear people really working on their issues and learn more about me. AA members used alcohol and drugs and I used food and sex. We shared the same issues, just different 'medicines'. I attended one meeting in Los Angeles in the early mornings and would see an angel appear in the back of the room from time to time. One morning I was going to skip the meeting but knew it was best I go. I was out of control and needed a safe place.

That day the angel appeared at the door next to me and we spoke briefly and exchanged names and kept glancing at each other with smiles that could light up a room. After the meeting we went across the street for tea and toast. I remember her having jam on her toast with coffee and I had tea. We laughed and both knew that moment that something was special between us, in our own worlds. You could feel the pull physically even if you were not near us. I walked Carla to her car and we agreed to see each other that night.

Once we got to her car around the corner from the meeting we held each other in our arms. The emotional connection at that moment was new to me. I felt safe and cared for. It was the first time that had happened to me. It was an emotion I have not felt since that day. We kissed and almost ripped our clothes off right there in the parking lot. Part of me was so excited to see her in my arms naked and sweaty and the other part really looked at her as the person I wanted to share my life with. Not just the sex, but who and what I was at that time. Funny how we want something so badly that we forget the reality right around the corner.

Our first date was magical in many ways. We had a great sushi dinner and strolled through Pasadena, California, looking at shops and watching people. I should have known that I was not really being honest with myself when I thought this was the one woman for me. Once we got to her house we had sex before we even went into her bedroom. Right there in the living room, out of lust. We both had no boundaries that night. From that point on for a short period of time until we moved in together the sex was very strong between us. It fed a loneliness we had in wanting to believe it was real. I knew that we both loved each other in a certain way, but I knew it was not a love like a man and woman share in an intimate relationship because, to this day, I do not think we *liked* each other.

What I saw in her was a warm and loving woman who needed someone to battle her fear of being alone. In my own life at this time I was still in my disease of food addiction. I wanted to make our relationship work, but I knew in my heart that I was not able to love me at all, let alone Carla. I told her this a short time after I moved in and continued to tell her that I could not love her as she needed and wanted. The relationship was so dysfunctional that we never really spoke about anything that mattered in life. We argued and fought so much it was draining and sad. I cried so many nights sitting on the couch talking with her and letting her know I did not want to be there.

It became such a habit to focus on our relationship rather than on my own needs that everything became mechanical and stagnant. In the bedroom we had stopped even touching each other, because I hated my body and felt so fat and ugly that I did not want her to even touch me. I tried to explain to her but she would not listen nor could she understand. The shame and embarrassment I felt were so deep that I could not tell her how much I hated my body. I had also lost interest in her sexually because sex became the same boring motions over and over. It was mainly my own issues with sex that stopped our intimacy from ever going further. I had no way of expressing how I felt, because it was new to me to even share my feelings and emotions with a woman. My emotional issues and addictions as well as Carla's dysfunctional life stopped us from having a chance to work things out.

I knew that it was over one night when we had just finished a very brief intimate moment and Carla started to cry. I asked what was wrong and she told me she just wanted someone to love her. Hell, I was right there and she wanted anyone. I tried for so long to love her as she wanted, and at the same time she could not love because she still had not dealt with so many issues from her past. After this night I retreated even more, emotionally and physically.

We were so dysfunctional that the only way we really communicated was through a make believe little girl named Darla that Carla did a voice for. Darla called me uncle Denny and I would talk to her and ask her to tell Aunt Carla whatever bothered me and Carla would have her do the same thing. This was not healthy, but it worked in our little distorted world. This child who never existed healed many lonely moments for us together.

During this time with Carla I was able to really see how I continued to attract women who had the same dysfunctional needs and lifestyles. I knew from the beginning that it was not a positive choice, as it had not been with Cindy. But, it fit into my needs at that time and into a pattern of dealing with others who, like me, did not want to really accept responsibility for their actions, thoughts, and behaviors. I left both relationships with scars, as did Carla and Cindy.

My scars were created by my need to believe that I was capable of making things work between myself and these women. It was my fear of being alone that kept me hanging in there no matter the emotional tug of war I faced every day. I learned that I really wanted to look at myself and what I needed, before I ever tried to create a life with someone again. I became honest as to why I wanted a relationship and what my part was in the whole picture.

In both of these relationships, I knew that I loved them and they loved me in the only way we knew how at the time. Though dysfunctional, that love was the warm blanket that kept us together until it was not possible to continue. I knew that the shame and disgust I had for my body and myself because of my addictions played a large part in the demise of my relationships. On the one hand,

Cindy and I went at it like animals without boundaries. With Carla it was just the opposite. From one extreme to another; that is how I handled everything back then. To this day I still have moments that I feel ugly, fat, disgusting, and not worthy of a woman's love. Now I know how to work through these moments and deal with why I feel this way. Whether it be the fear of intimacy or of sharing who I really am, I look at why I react and then what is positive and negative before I make decisions.

In these relationships I did not trust Cindy or Carla for many reasons. Cindy was always trying to get me to be jealous of other men. I would tell her just to shower before she got into bed, if that was what she wanted to do with other men. With Carla it seemed at all times that she loved me only because I was filling a void in her life. She could always find fault in others without ever being responsible for her own part in situations. But I have no regrets. As with business, you learn what you need and want for success and I think you learn this in relationships. I now trust myself, so I can trust others without assuming they will lie or deceive me. It is funny and I believe this, when we point the finger at others it usually is because we are the one who is guilty. This is true in my life in many situations.

In 1998 I met the first woman with whom I had a functional or mutually respectful relationship. I was in a restaurant in Pasadena and sat in Nicole's section for dinner. I had noticed her before, with her infectious smile, bright eyes, and wonderful peacefulness. I lived in downtown Los Angeles in a high-rise artist community. I had a great 2,500 square foot space that was the dream place I had wanted for years. I never had the chance to really spend much time there, but I was proud of myself for having my own place and paying for it legally. I was working at Anacapa By The Sea, in Port Hueneme, California, to open an eating disorder unit. Seeing Nicole each time I ate in the restaurant brought a smile to my face. I finally decided after eating there so many times just to see her just to ask her out, and she accepted to my delight. This was so different for me. I was nervous about it and felt like a kid at his first school dance. Once I asked her out, I felt as though 10 tons of self-inflicted pressure had been removed from my head.

Nicole and I spent many hours on the telephone talking and laughing about anything and everything. There was attraction but not dysfunction as it had been with Cindy and Carla. Nicole was the type of woman I really respected and admired. She was college educated, worked at her career, compassionate, and emotionally healthy, as healthy as one could be. We had different backgrounds, family structure, goals, and ideas. We learned and shared so much together that it was the first time I had someone in my life who really could be a positive addition to my life. The best thing about this relationship was that it progressed slowly and we did not jump into a sexual encounter as I had before with everyone else. We did not even kiss for almost three months! The relationship was built on a friendship before anything else. Nicole was the one woman I knew I could talk to and not be judged. In fact, she loved to hear about my past. I had to be honest and open and I liked that about her. No bullshit or just small talk. I looked forward to seeing her and being with her.

This relationship had its sexual side, but we never consummated the relationship because I did not feel it would be right due to our lifestyles at that time. I had gone to Florida in May of 1998 to help restructure a nonprofit eating disorder association (IAEDP, International Association of Eating Disorder Professionals) and that move put a lot of stress on our relationship. I chose to go without ever discussing this with her and it was a decision I made. Now I know that if I have a partner in life everything has to be discussed and compromises reached or the relationship will not work.

We talked all the time while I was in Florida, and I missed her even more than I ever missed any woman. She came to visit. It was a little odd for both of us because we had not seen each other in four months, but we dealt with it. The magic we felt at the start of our relationship was gone and much of that was due to being apart. I went back and forth between California and Florida and would always stay with her. We would have fun, but it was cold. We discussed consummating the relationship but I told her at that time it would mean more to her than to me and would not be fair to her. If I was going any farther sexually I wanted to be there with her in California. The relationship ended in part because I would not have sex and because we had grown apart. It was hard for me but it was a wonderful experience that I have never forgotten. I know I can have a healthy relationship and I know what one is like. I look forward to that time when it will be right for me and that special person. Nicole was a gift from God who taught me it was okay to love and to be loved no matter what happens. As with any relationship we had to work on things, but it was worth every moment. If she reads this, I hope she knows I really loved her like no other woman.

Today I have a great relationship with who I am and what I *need* in my life from a partner, as opposed to what I *want*. I have forgiven and accepted myself for who and what I am today. My past is always part of me, but it is not who I am any more. I am free from assumptions of what may happen in life, and I live each day thirsty for what it brings and who it brings into my life. My higher power lights each step I take. I no longer feel fear of sharing who I was or who I am, because I do not control what others will think – nor do I want to exercise such control any more. I am happy and always growing, thanks to these wonderful women who I had the opportunity to be with and learn from.

Chapter Twelve: Sex Addiction

"Are you sure it will be okay to spend Thanksgiving at your mom's place?" I asked Gwen as I poured her a drink. It was three days before Thanksgiving in 1987. I was bartending at The Palladium, a nightclub in New York City. I had been there for a while and it was a great and cozy place. A friend and I had gone there one Friday night to dance, five months before I met Gwen. We danced all night on these huge speakers and this little old guy asked to speak with us after he had observed us for a while. We found out later that he was the owner, Steve Rubell of Studio 54 fame, and he offered us bartending jobs. We had heard about him and thought he was just drunk that night. A manager came over and gave us a time to be there the following day for an interview. I thought what the hell, we could make a lot of money and have fun. Little did I know it would fuel the dysfunctional lifestyle I led – and so desired – even more.

I had met Gwen three weeks earlier and gone back to her apartment for a wild night of sex that did not stop until the next day. She was nineteen years old and mature in every way beyond her years. When I first met her she said she was twenty-two and a student at New York University studying photography. I found out her real age later in our friendship. Gwen was 5'4", with very large firm breasts and a beautiful body as well. She was very sexual and had no problems doing anything sexual at any place or at any time. We had no inhibitions while we were together and no expectations from one another. We had spent three or four nights a week together since we met. We both liked the other's sexual appetite and knew we were seeing other people. Her apartment was near mine so it was easy to meet up after work.

One of the other women I had been seeing at this time, Mary, had called me earlier in the day to invite me to Thanksgiving dinner with her and her daughter on the Upper East Side. She was divorced and 20 years older than me but looked as if she was 25 years old. We had a lot of fun, not looking for anything else from each other. Her daughter was at school and would be home for the holiday. Mary always came to the club and then we would go to my place. We could not wait to ravish each other when I got off work. The 15-minute taxi ride was too long.

I weighed both offers and since I had already accepted Mary's invitation I made plans with Gwen to see a movie after dinner. Gwen was into bondage, exhibitionism, porn, girls, and role-playing. We did it all. I thought it would be fun to see both of them that day and feast on all the food and both of these beautiful sexy women. We agreed to meet at 9:30 at a Broadway movie house after we both had dinner with friends.

I was excited to see Mary because it had been a while since we had been together. She had been out of town and I had never been to her apartment. Mary was a regular who came in every Friday and Saturday night for over six months. We started by just talking and having fun and exploring the Palladium for places to have sex while I worked. It was what it was. I did not know what she did for a living or anything about her daughter or past husband. What I knew about her and what she knew about me was perfect for each of us. Before she left on her trip we had been spending Friday and Saturday nights at my place for almost three months straight. She always left real early and that fit perfectly for both of us.

Mary asked me to come for dinner at 4:30. That was a great time because I had called in sick to work and it gave me plenty of time to eat and spend time with Mary and still get to a movie to see Gwen.

I bought some flowers to take to Mary and upon arriving at her apartment I had one thing on my mind and it was not dinner. I wanted to walk in the door and take her the minute I saw her, but I knew her daughter would be there. As I rang the bell I waited for a few moments and the door opened. I stood in shock, disbelief, confusion, and was excited and aroused. I was looking right into Gwen's eyes. We both froze and all I could hear was Mary heading to the hallways to greet me and introduce her daughter to me. As Mary approached I looked at Gwen to see her reaction and she started to giggle and I began to smile. Mary introduced us, then gave me a kiss on the mouth and grabbed my crotch as Gwen turned to lead me into the living room. Later I found out that Gwen had seen her grab me. Part of me wanted to just leave and the other part felt as if this was going to be something to remember. I was calm and did not think twice about the situation. The only way Mary would know about Gwen and me was if Gwen told her.

We walked into the living room to sit down as Mary went to the kitchen to get something to drink for all of us. As I sat there Gwen looked at me with a sly smile, then headed into the kitchen with her mom. They were in there for what seemed like an eternity, but returned in a few minutes. My mind was racing with all kinds of scenarios as they re-entered the room. I did not know what they spoke about and did not ask.

After some small talk we sat down for dinner at the table with so much sexual tension it could only be cut with a power saw. When one got up to use the restroom or get something from the kitchen I would kiss and fondle the other and vice-versa. It was fun and the high was out of this world. Mary knew I had to leave by 9 p.m. and Gwen told her mom that plans with friends had been cancelled. After dinner it was time for dessert and I declined. Mary asked me again and I declined more than once. I was afraid to eat even a small piece of pumpkin pie in front of anyone. Gwen told me the dessert was out of this world and it was best with whipped cream. Finally after saying no I agreed to one bite. Both Gwen and Mary went into the kitchen and Gwen returned with a can of whipped cream.

As she walked toward me she held out her hand for me to take. I took her hand and she led me down the hall to Mary's master bedroom. I stood there without saying a word and she closed the door half way. Gwen informed me that she was the first serving of dessert tonight and that the second helping would soon follow. I sat on the edge of the bed and Gwen turned the stereo on to slow sexy music and began a slow and sexy striptease for me. She sat facing me on my lap and placed the whipped cream in her nipples for me to gently dissolve with my mouth. As we lay in bed exploring our bodies as we had many times before I felt a hand on my leg that I knew was not Gwen's. As I looked over my shoulder I noticed Mary standing in a very sexy matching bra and panties. She was as stunning as always and she proceeded to join her daughter and me. I do not want to get graphic, but I did not leave Mary's apartment until the following evening. It was a night that we would re-enact on three more occasions while continuing to see each other separately over the next year. We never discussed this because we never thought twice about it. Gwen and Mary never performed any sexual acts on each other. They liked the situation and saw nothing wrong with what we did. This was my world of sex and welcome to it. It only got crazier as time went on.

From the moment Richard Savala showed me a porn magazine in the back of our fourth grade class room at Holy Cross Grade School when I was nine years old, I have been fascinated with the female body and with women. The pure beauty of a woman excites me in every way. The way women walk, their clothes, smiles, hair, voices, sexy shoes, hands, bodies, compassion, and intellect are pure magic to me. From that moment on I was mesmerized and wanted to know more about the female body and what women needed and wanted both emotionally and sexually. Since I did not date until my junior year in high school, I continued to dream and fantasize about the touch of a woman and a gentle kiss. Once I looked at the pictures in that magazine, I became obsessed with seeing more. I would always look at these books in the porn magazine section at stores and cover them up by placing them in a sports book so no one could see what I was reading.

I did not want to get caught by the workers at the stores or by my mom or grandma. I had no one telling me about sex or answering my questions. I realized I had to learn on my own, but it was not a healthy way to learn – for a fourth grader or an adult. The schools never discussed sex, and having no male figure in my life made it hard for my mom to talk to me. She never tried and I do not blame her. My sexual education was to come from porn magazines, books on sex, massage parlor telephone conversations, and experimenting with my neighbor girlfriend when we were 10 years old.

I lived in Bryte, California, when I was 10, in an old house not far from my grade school. Our neighbors seemed like nice people but I never got to know the adults, just the kids. They had one son my age and a daughter who was a year younger. The son was not athletic and seemed not to want to play much, so the little girl and I played a lot. We were always talking and just sharing innocent moments. We would hug each other at times, but there was nothing to it.

One day we were playing in her backyard and she asked me to show her my penis, and if I did she would show me her private part, as she called it. I was stunned and looked around because I did not know what to say or do. I had seen women nude in the magazines but never someone my age. It seemed harmless at that moment. That day we did not play show and tell, we talked about it and planned to do it when the time was right. We did not want to get caught or in trouble. We agreed to wait two more days until we knew our parents were at work and then we would meet behind the garage.

I had on my salt and pepper pants and white uniform shirt from school because I had just gotten home. She had on a little skirt and tee shirt. I hurried to my room to put my stuff away and looked out the window to see her heading out the back door of her house. I was excited but did not want to run out the door so I told my grandma I was just going to play with my neighbor in the yard. We met behind the garage as planned. I arrived just as she began to sit on the steps leading into the garage back door. As she stood up we both froze and just stared. She had her hair fixed differently from what it usually was and I was excited and nervous. We knew we could be punished if caught, but we didn't care.

We looked at each other to see who would make the first move. We talked and agreed at the count of three I would unzip my pants and she would lift her skirt. She counted and at three we did as we had agreed. We both stood looking very puzzled and curious. She had her panties down around her knees. She did not look like the pictures I had seen before and I did not know what she was thinking. We moved closer to look without saying anything. After a few minutes we laughed an odd laugh, then fixed our clothes and agreed to meet the next day. I went home and could not stop thinking about seeing her and what we would do the next day.

I did not know what to do even if I wanted to do something. After meeting on the fifth straight day we discussed going farther than just looking. We agreed to touch each other with our hands. She went first and just held my penis in her hand and then looked at me as she was holding it. She stepped back and I put my hand between her legs to feel her and it was odd but exciting. After our explorations we sat and talked about everything but what had just happened. We then did something we never even talked about. We kissed. It was awkward and goofy. Our mouths were closed and our eyes were shut as well. When we moved in to kiss we almost bloodied our lips because we could not see each other. It hurt a little, but we stopped and tried it with our eyes open. There was no big rush physically, but it was fun.

At this time in my life I was very interested in the female body and mine as well. I had read an article at the store on how men and women masturbated. I know now that it was just a porn magazine and it was very graphic. It detailed how a man and woman sat across from each other on a bed and reached orgasm as the other watched. I kind of understood it and tried it myself. It was odd but felt great when it was over. I always got an erection when I saw half naked women or the porn magazines. The erection was odd because I did not really know what to do. Once I read the article I knew for the erection to go away I just needed to masturbate, so I did. The stories and pictures never failed to get me excited. I had no one to share these feelings with or to ask questions of because I knew I would get in trouble from reading the books. The fear of getting caught reading the books did not stop me. It excited me more than anything.

My neighbor and I continued this secret for almost two months until one afternoon when it all came to an end in one horrifying moment. On that day we met as usual behind the garage, but this time we met later than we always had. Since the time had changed we did not know if anyone would see us or find us so we agreed to play real fast and then continue the following day. We talked a little and then agreed to play our show and tell real quick.

As I began to pull my pants down and she began to lift her dress and pull her panties down, her father came out of nowhere from around the corner. We had no idea he was even home. It was still before 5:00 and that was the time he usually came home. He dropped a can of beer he had in his left hand and froze. As he looked at us we did not move or even breathe, we froze as well. I will never forget the look of shock and fear on her face. I was afraid but more afraid for her. Her father always had a temper and we could hear him at night screaming at his wife and kids. She was afraid of her father, as was the rest of the family.

Without notice he lunged toward her and grabbed her by the arm before she had a chance to even pull up her panties. I pulled my pants up as fast as I could and stood there. Her father began to shake her without mercy and her head and body went in opposite directions with each violent shake. I stood frozen in fear for her and did not know what I could do. He started slapping her about the face, body, and butt. She and I were both crying now. With each explosion he called her a whore, a slut, and a good-for-nothing-bitch. He told her she was going to hell and then he stopped shaking her and her body fell limp to the ground.

As she lay there he turned suddenly to me as I watched her cry and he placed large calloused hands on my shoulders and squeezed so hard that later I had bruises. She was sitting on the ground yelling through her tears that she was sorry and to stop, please. He pulled me closer until I could feel the spit from his mouth and he looked me in the eyes and told me what we were doing was filthy, dirty, and disgusting, and that I was going to hell as well.

I did not know what he was going to do next to either one of us. As she sat there my heart beat so fast I thought it was going to pop out of my chest. After yelling at me, he did not let go. I stood frozen as my friend got up off the ground and grabbed her dad's arm and yelled for him to let go. He shoved her to the ground and threw me back against a fence that was near the garage back door. There was a hole in the fence farther down near the end of the property that I always used to get into their back yard. I wanted to run to that hole but I could not move. He looked as if he had calmed down because he was no longer yelling and his eyes did not look blank. Suddenly he grabbed her by the top of her head with a hand full of hair and began to drag her around the corner of the garage. She kept begging him to let go and we were both crying and yelling at him. He stopped and took a step toward me and I froze. I did not know if he was going to hurt me or not. He yelled at me to get out of his yard or I would get what was coming to me. We were crying as he pulled her into the house. I walked slowly then sprinted to the hole in the fence and ran to my bedroom. I looked out the window but couldn't see anything in their windows. I sat in the corner and cried.

I was so scared I never mentioned this to my family, out of fear of punishment and the fact that maybe I was going to hell. Did I do something wrong? I did not know. He made me feel dirty and disgusting. I never discussed this until I was in my thirties. I knew we had not done anything wrong but did not know who to talk to.

My neighbor and I saw each other from time to time over the next four months but we never spoke. I knew the punishment was harsh for her and the guilt I had carried because that bastard hurt her was more than I could handle. Her father spoke to my mom and grandma, but I don't think he ever said anything to them about the incident. Four months after that day my neighbors moved. I never had a chance to say goodbye or that I was sorry. To this day I do not know what happened to her or her family.

My first sexual encounter was mired in violence and verbal abuse from an adult who said I was going to hell. Being a young boy and at Catholic school, I really thought I might be. I tried to put this behind me for years, but it was never to be. Not speaking to someone out of fear and shame pushed this episode into the dark and dangerous side of sexual desires that I would later experience in life. I punished myself for this. That punishment almost killed me.

From that time until I entered high school I would fantasize about my encounter with my neighbor and the excitement of being caught. Not excitement for what her father did, but we both knew we could be seen at any time and we still played our game. I masturbated to the memories of us and the women I read about and their pictures. It seemed as if I masturbated in places where I could be caught at any time, school, public bathrooms, restaurants, but I never got caught. My bathroom and bedroom were the two main places. The idea of placing a face into a story came in handy when I got older and began having sex for money. Many times I hated what I was doing and was not attracted to the woman in front of me. The money and power gave me the high but I always dreamed of someone else while I completed the task at hand. In reality no one was in control. All anyone ever did was to pay me to leave. That is what prostitution is about in my view.

I remember in high school everyone made fun of me, both boys and girls, because I was a big kid who wore thick black glasses and had short hair. I was not popular at all until my junior year. I did not look at the girls in high school as sexual when I first arrived as a freshman. I wanted the women in the magazines, not some little girl who was still physically and emotionally immature. I liked to think of the women in the stories and what they meant by certain things they did with men and for men and other women. I wanted to be the person they did these things with. I did not know what oral sex, bondage, orgasm, or a threesome meant. I learned later and it was everything I wanted and everything that numbed me to real sex and intimacy. I learned more about my body and what felt good to me as time went on. I never shared this with anyone because I had no friends in high school and no adult to talk to.

In my junior year girls started to talk to me and show an interest in me. I was excited and nervous because I did not know how to react to them. During my first two years I always wanted to be liked by girls and it did not happen. One year I went to a dance and asked eight girls to dance and they all said no. The pain and humiliation of boys and girls laughing was something I did not wish on my enemies. I took all that abuse and remembered how it felt later in life. I made up for their cruel comments and all the laughter when a girl turned me down. I had more sex than imaginable in order to feel okay after all those years of being rejected. Later on in life, sex became as easy for me as breathing. I was okay with being the guy who had little talent in sports but more heart and passion than anyone else. I was someone who did not give up. I knew I was not going to be accepted or liked by girls. But in my junior year it changed. I got contact lenses and that made a big difference after basketball season. I did not have the big thick glasses any more. I felt different and looked different.

It felt so incredible to be noticed by girls as something other than a kid who ate a lot or was just a big guy who was into sports. I started dating Katie my junior year and I felt so high to have a girlfriend. She attended St. Francis High School, an all girls school in Sacramento, California. I felt a fear of losing her, which did happen my senior year.

From our first kiss it was pure pleasure. In addition to being with her, the sexual arousal was strong. I did not have to fantasize any more. I was experiencing contact with a real woman. It was so intense that the summer between my junior and senior year I would walk three quarters of a mile to her house early in the mornings. No matter how tired I was I knew when I got there we would sneak upstairs and explore each other's bodies with great anticipation and excitement. It became something that I dreamed of at night, waiting for the morning to come.

When we were at her house we also spent time upstairs away from her parents and the thought of getting caught was always in my mind and that was exciting to me. We stumbled during our sexual moments but we learned and that was special to me. Katie never had a negative thing to say about our sexual relationship and it was mutual. It was great to feel wanted as a person and sexually.

Chapter Thirteen: Spirituality

From my readings and understanding of the Bible and other religious books, I believe that God sent Jesus here with many obstacles in his way to re-form men and women into a unity of one. We believe we are supposed to live a lifestyle conducive to love and compassion for others – and for ourselves – regardless of color, religious beliefs, economic background, education levels, sexual orientation, or any other superficial differences. I believe in a God who placed the obstacles here and still chose to come and show us that we could change others by examples of compassion, truth, honesty, and faith.

I have had a very defined and personal relationship with my own spirituality and what spirituality means to me. This began when I was at Holy Cross grade school in Bryte, California. In the belief system that I have come to trust and depend upon in times of fear, happiness, loneliness, anger, depression, joy, and need, I have learned that the more compassion I have for myself, the more I have peace in my faith and in my choices, thoughts, ideas, and actions. This extends to other people and recognizing their needs and wants as well.

In fourth grade, Sister Cathleen suspended me after an incident in church that helped define my belief and trust in God and spirituality. I was talking with other children in the pew and Sister was sitting behind us. After a while she approached me, grabbed my arm, and told me that my behavior was inappropriate in church and my talking upset the other kids. Mind you, this was while we were all talking to each other. Then she hit me with a verbal bomb that I have never forgotten: She said that I had ruined her day with God and that what I had done was unforgivable. I was scared and afraid of getting into trouble with my mom, our priest at that time, Father Casper, or the Big Guy Upstairs.

Sister Cathleen, with my arm in her vice-like grip, escorted me out of the church in front of all the students and teachers. The guilt and shame I felt was evident as I walked out with my head down. I felt the eyes of everybody on me while they snickered at me. I got caught and they did not.

Despite the humiliation, what made the day so special was that I learned something that helped shape my belief in God and my spiritual connection with God. One, talking in school was not good for me and it did have an effect on others. Even more important was the fact that Sister and Father Casper were representatives of God to me, but the ways they treated me were completely opposite. Sister blamed and shamed me into thinking God was upset with me, and that I had to look for a way to gain His forgiveness and trust, as well as earning her trust again. Father Casper told me what I had done was wrong, but that God accepts us all for whom we are, and that sometimes people like the Sister get carried away. There I was with two representatives of God with contradictory positions. (I learned later it was the old good cop – bad cop routine.)

What I realized was that they were people just like me, people who each chose a vocation for personal reasons – they needed to feel closer to God or serve His purposes here on Earth. They interpreted what they read in the Bible, as most people do, in light of what they were taught, so they could carry the word of God as they saw it to those they served. The important word here is *served*.

If I am here to serve others, and I believe I have been chosen to serve, how can I judge or condemn Sister Cathleen or Father Casper? I believe that religion is man-made and that spirituality is God-given. God gave us all the ability to have compassion, for ourselves and for others. We are supposed to share and lead by example.

As a young child I lacked spirituality because I did not believe anything good was ever going to happen after all the family strife and pain I went through. If God so loved the world (and me), then why did he let this happen? I know it was a test, to show me how strong I could be and that I could make changes. Believing is half the battle. It's scary to believe we make a difference, but we do.

In 1994, I realized that I couldn't rely on other humans to make decisions for me. Reliance on others for making my decisions was not justified by my fear or my failure to take responsibility. Now, when I make choices I feel strong and serene, that everything is okay no matter what the outcome may be from those choices. I have learned that the choices I make are part of my spiritual being and I alone reap the consequences, positive or negative. The question is whether or not anything is *really* negative. I don't believe so. I use everything now as a learning experience for those I reach out to and for myself. I lead by example and from personal experience.

By trusting my identity – how I am and my choices – I am letting go of all the fear that used to surround every decision I made. I no longer fear my choices or worry. My fear kept me from growing spiritually and progressing in life. Fear is healthy – up to a point; it keeps us alive in dangerous situations. However, I now have a healthy fear, with boundaries about dealing with fear and overcoming the things that used to cripple me in the past.

I do not need to see anything concrete. I just need to know it works, it is there, and all will be fine. It has certainly been scary, but this has been a journey that I would never have wanted to miss. Spirituality is a feeling of knowing you make the right decisions for yourself and for the betterment of others. I have done that now. This chapter is short because I am not here to preach, only to tell you what works for me. If what you are doing in your own life is not working, give this a try. The only thing we ever have to lose is time itself, and we have plenty of that. Find out who you are, not what you are, and you will find the spirituality you seek – or have avoided. Live your life in compassion for others and yourself.

Chapter Fourteen: Honor Thyself

Honesty has been the one thing that has been a constant on my path through recovery. It has not been easy to always be honest with myself about who and what I am or who I was in the past. However, I have been able to grow to the person I am today because I do not lie to myself any more.

My recovery process, as with so many others who have braved this winding road through hell and back, was very painful and at the same time the greatest journey I had ever undertaken. During this journey I struggled to hold myself accountable and responsible for everything I said and did to myself or others. The fear factor was off the charts, but, with each open and honest moment, I created positive habits that now allow me the peace I had long sought in my past through food, sex, prostitution, lying, stealing, manipulating, and anything else to numb the pain. Knowing that I was able to hide behind my addictions made it so easy to just stay within my own little world – and it was *little* – rather than face the truth and explore what was out there for me in the big, real world. My comfort zone was my body and nothing else. It would have been so easy to stay sick and dysfunctional in my tiny world, but I would have been dead by now, either emotionally or physically.

My final journey to recovery began in 1994 with my last stay in a rehabilitation center in Southern California. The one thing I was more afraid of than anything else was what Jeff Radant had told me when we first met during this stay. Jeff asked me to tell the truth during our first meeting and I thought that, even though I was in a rehab and they where there to help me, he would think I was a freak, a loser, unworthy of love, a pathetic excuse for a human being. I thought I had to lie to him to be accepted, so I lied – which to me was like breathing. In my mind if he really knew me he would loathe me. In reality, I was the only one who did that to me – and I did it very well. While speaking with Jeff Radant and some of the other therapists, I was able to really open up after a while and discuss things without guilt, shame, or verbal abuse thrown back at me. For the first time in my life, people were speaking *to* me rather than *at* me. Jeff Radant and Jeff Schwartz, the director of the facility, let me know it was OK to talk about things I had always feared. I knew that I had no more chances or excuses to stay in my little world without dying.

The truth I had been seeking without fear of self-ridicule or judgment of others came to me as I continued to look at myself through the eyes of an honest man I had never really known before – me. I saw that I *could* live without my eating disorder being the answer to my underlying issues, pain, and fear. The hard part was to put what I had seen into action. I learned from Jeff R. and Jeff S. how to look at situations and handle them from a positive and realistic point of view, rather than turning to food, sex, or the other dysfunctional behaviors I turned to as treatment for my emotional pain. But, even though I learned these great tools to use, each day it was very hard and painful to implement the new boundaries I needed to overcome years and years of dysfunctional coping skills and habits. It was going to take time and I knew it.

Since I was a child I have known that a *process* had to occur before change could happen. I learned this from observing my family and other families while growing up. To make that process successful I would have to change from the warm insulated world I had created to the cold hard reality of the real world I never wanted to be a part of.

While in my last stay with both Jeffs – individuals I could look up to and trust – I knew that my paranoia over body image issues was the one constant that led me to relapse over and over and over. Food was the numbing mechanism for self-hate and doubt. The fear I had about food was so strong that it blocked me from learning anything from what they told me in the beginning of my stay. I shut them out 95% of the time, and gradually let in their words and adapted them to cope while in a rehab with 20-plus other people. I knew, at times, there was hope for me, but making the changes I needed seemed so far from reality that it was easier to take steps back rather than to go forward. I let in what they said. It slowly made sense – if I was to recover. What they said was so logical, but horrifying to think about trying. Being the control freak I was, I wanted to be the one to save my ass – not some strangers. But these strangers were angels.

The distorted image I had about my body and what it needed to look like was so delusional that it fed the need for the enormous amounts of food I put into my body to numb the pain of seeing the horrible disgusting person I saw as me. As I could not see reality, the positive information I was receiving was not registering in my brain or allowing me to process it so I could make the healthy choices I so wanted.

It took from my first day in rehab, July 15, 1994, until September of 1997 to pave the path I needed to get to the wonderful life I have today. The process was full of ups, downs, and of many of the same scenarios I had faced when sick, the difference being that I had positive actions I could realistically understand, choose, and carry out. I learned that the old quick-fix ways had to be put aside in order to get to where I wanted to be. I am where I am today because I worked at my issues and problems and overcame the destructive behavior and actions of the past. I now see the problem, face it, and find a solution. This has always been a challenge, but once I overcame my fear I was able to move forward.

I have read many books about people who suffer from different afflictions and many seem to say they are "cured" or "everything is OK". I think that's great. But it can be a trap when we do not deal honestly with reality. I know that the life I live today is due to my dealing with reality and the truth. I have depressed days, hard days, ugly days, want-to-eat-everything-in-sight days, but I do not fool myself by thinking that my past behaviors and actions are the answer. Abusing food, sex, or any of my numbing games as medicine to cure my emotional pain is no longer an option. It did not work then, and sure as hell will never work now. I face adversity with honesty.

During my last stay in rehab, I was introduced to the 12-step program called Overeaters Anonymous ("OA") designed for those of us who suffered from this silent killer. It was my first time attending meetings and I did not gel at all with the other members or the ideas presented. Now, do not get me wrong, and, please, do not think negatively about OA. It is a wonderful organization and I still attend meetings, because any help is better than just trying to fight alone when in an emotional crisis. However, I needed something more concrete, something that was going to hold me accountable and responsible for my behaviors and actions.

The meetings I first went to were all women and young girls – maybe a man once in a while. In these meetings, I was looked at as an outsider. Some questioned if I was actually sick. Some women even thought I was there to meet someone to date. If you need to go to meetings where others are sick as you to find your dream person, then you are really in trouble. It is like going from the fire to the oven. Keep choosing the wrong people to follow and learn from, and you will always be where you do not want to be – sick. These groups are great for support, but do not use them to fulfill the emptiness you have inside. That can and must be filled by yourself.

One important thing about recovery is that there is no one way to do it for everyone. Our paths are similar, but we all have to make choices that help us or not. OA kept me in limbo. The motto of "keep coming back" when I did not see or hear recovery was very disappointing and sad. I wanted something stronger, with more structure, something that would say to me, "You are the reason and the answer," and I was.

In some OA meetings, women went as far as to ask me to leave because they had issues with men in their lives and a man in group was hard for them to deal with. I understood but I stayed, because I was there for me. I was confused because here was an organization that was for everyone, but that many inside tried to make into something else. Many people believe that *OA* tells you not to eat sugar and such, when in reality it is the members of a group who create rules for their own meetings, not OA dictating what you can and cannot eat.

My truth is that *I* saved my life with the help of others who loved and cared for me. Not a group of like minded people such as OA. I applaud all who go to meetings, because it takes courage and conviction to get help and expose ourselves to total strangers no matter how much we have in common. I say this because we tend to give credit to other people rather than to ourselves, which makes it easier to blame that person or group when things don't work out. To get to where I am today, I had to make myself responsible for me at all times and take the blame and the praise for what I do in my life. It works if you are willing to be honest.

I created the amazing life I have today on a foundation of truth and honesty toward my needs and wants in life. I no longer bullshit myself into thinking all will be fine. I take action and positive things happen.

While in rehab in 1994 and trying to deal with the OA situation, I wrote down some points that, if I followed them, I knew would make a difference in my life and allow me the serenity I so desired. I wrote down ideas and thoughts as to what I needed to do to get through each day without someone else doing it for me. These thoughts became *The Daily Process, 16 Points to Life*©. Once I was able to use these *Points* in situations that I faced after rehab, I learned that I could make the difference. It was up to me and no one else. These *Points* are not just for someone who suffers an eating disorder or another addiction. They are for those who need to be accountable for their lives, and who want to make changes. By following the *Points*, I was able to gain more insight into who I am, and understand why I used food and other things as coping mechanisms to numb my pain.

Each of us can use these *Points* to change the person we are into the person we were meant to be:

1. I admitted I had no power to do it alone and it was OK to ask for help.

2. I looked at my past and realized I was never in control.

3. I always hurried to get from one point or place to the next, never realizing that I just walked away.

4. I always wanted to help others – it let me hide from the reality of my own life.

5. Each time I thought I had it all – career, money, health, and love – I couldn't hold on because I had no bond with my higher power.

6. I cared for many in my own way. Now, I see the dysfunction I paved on my path for help.

7. I asked for forgiveness from those I hurt; many laughed, some understood. I respect their feelings either way, but now I respect mine.

8. Each day before was filled with empty time. Through my learning process I have structure to aid my day and mind.

9. The temptation to return to my past because it was so safe, I thought, will not go away without my belief in me and love for who I am.

10. I've forgiven myself for what I appeared to be.

11. I can now give to those who want a better life, with boundaries I set. Those who are not ready, I can only help them with what they can see in their attempt for serenity.

12. Tasks left undone from my list each day means only that I now have to find the time to do them when the time is right. I do not have to be angry or abusive to myself because I feel as if I have failed. I have not failed. I have succeeded to the best of my ability today.

13. My self-respect and confidence are being restored each and every day. I remember the past and how nothing would ever last.

14. I now look in the mirror and the monster has been put to sleep, but I know if I slip off track it will conquer me when weak.

15. Each day now I look at my future. I see that my past has helped me get to where I am now, but my abstinence is where I want and need to be.

16. Once I turned my life over to my own "HP" (higher power), I saw how it helped me get through the past, is guiding in the present, and will be there in my future.

At first it was hard to follow these *Points*, and it took me three years to cement the points into my daily life without fear, shame, guilt, or anxiety about my past indiscretions, while feeling positive and confident in my choices due to the freedom the *16 Points* brought into my life. I did it – no one else – and that feeling is second to none.

The process of writing these *Points* was painful and liberating at the same time, and my emotions ran from high to lower than an ant. I kept thinking, "What would people say about these *Points*?" Would they say they were self-serving? Well, they were. I needed something for me – nothing else was helping. I did not write them with the intention of sharing them with others, but, as they did help create the balance and structure I have in my life today, I thought that others could benefit if they chose to adhere to the *The Daily Process, 16 Points to Life*©, as I have.

Change is do-able but not easy. If you want to change you can follow these *Points* and make a difference, rather than turning to someone or something else for the answers. The answers lie within us, and all we need is a little help to find the confidence on which to build our foundation.

When I went into rehab in 1994, I was scared to lose the one identity I had – my eating disorder. It gave me everything, and at the same time betrayed me every day. I thought that if I was not the "sick one", then who or what would I be? It was all I knew at that time. I cherished the fact that people knew me for my eating disorder, because there was no other way they could identify me. It was better than no one acknowledging me at all. I was somebody, at least in my distorted world.

As with so many of us when we look back at our lives, I see that my identity had always been attached to negativity and dysfunctional behaviors and actions: From the kid who ate so much in school so others would notice him and stop making fun of him for being poor or heavy or fatherless, to the adult who was a liar, cheat, thief, and manipulator.

In the past, I always crossed a line because it is what I chose to do – it was how I coped with life. It was always easier than really getting to know who I was, and what I needed in life to be happy and free from the emotional pain that thumped inside of my head every second of every day. When I decided to shed the labels that I lived by and cherished as my identity, it meant that I had to get to know the real me and not the one I let everyone see. By making this choice to be honest about who I was and what I was doing, I was forced to face the unknown. It was the scariest thing for me to do. But without facing *me,* I would have died a long time ago. I realized the unknown could not be any worse than what I did know and used to cure my problems. And I was right. Without living the pain, I would have not made it to where I am today – a healthy mind in a healthy body.

Once I started to work with the idea that the therapists knew more than I did at the time, and I began to trust their input into my life, I began to trust myself and how I really felt. It was amazing to feel that honesty without trying to numb it with food, sex, stealing, manipulation, prostitution, anger, or victimizing others to soothe my pain. The honesty I had never known began to come up in groups, with family and friends, with others, and most of all with me. This honesty was – and is – the major part of my recovery. Sitting there in groups and slowly discussing my issues with a mind open for feedback made it easier to confront my fears, shame, guilt, anger, low, low, low self-esteem, self-hatred, and lack of self-respect. I no longer believed I had to hide and numb my pain.

I learned in groups, through many tears and smiles, that, by allowing myself to make mistakes and learning to be accountable and responsible for what I had done to others and myself, I could overcome those mistakes and my fixation with perfection. Perfection only lasts for a split second and then anything can happen. I always thought I had to be perfect to get to the next level, and all that thinking led me deeper into the abyss I called life. I thought that a mistake meant failure, but in reality those mistakes were lessons. Today, I do not think in all-or-nothing or black-or-white thoughts.

The one thing that was really an eye opener for me in my last stay in rehab is that the people treating me were no healthier than I was. That was very scary. Some of the therapists had so many personal issues, that they brought them to work and projected them on to us patients. Knowing that these people had problems made it easier for me to deal with mine. It was like those of us who reach out to constantly help others so we do not have to deal with our own issues. I have found this true of over 50% of the professionals I have dealt with in the addiction field. Please, do not get me wrong. I am *not* saying they are not good at what they do. They are just like you and I, who suffer.

My last stay during rehab was a foundation building experience, both good and bad, for my recovery. Like so many others, I went into rehab knowing and I mean *knowing* that I knew it all and that the professionals there did not know jack shit. I acted put upon when asked to participate or express myself in a group or with a therapist in a one-on-one session. The truth was, I was scared to open up to others because I did not want them to know the real person behind the mask. I thought if they knew me, it would create more pain for me, because they would judge me harder than I judged myself. I kept up this lying to myself until Jeff Radant and Jeff Schwartz explained that I could continue my behaviors and actions and stay in my abyss or try slowly and with pain to open up to them and to the others in rehab. I tried their approach. It was not the torture I thought it would be. It was painful and scary and I dreaded every moment, but my only other option was to die a slow death without ever living life to the fullest. I had to remember that, in my world, I was always in control and called the shots no matter the outcome, *and that was not working* so I had nothing to lose by accepting others' help. I had thought for so long that by letting others in I was losing control of who I was. But I did not know who I was before I let others into my life to help me. Now I know who I am and what I am here to do. I am here to make a difference for people who are like me, and not just those who are addicts.

Once I started to share the truth about the pain and its origin, it became easier in groups to let myself go. People started to listen without judgment. They were like me and suffered the same problems, all to different degrees, so I felt I was not the freak I had always thought I was. We all had stories. But I was still nervous and scared, because in rehab it was a structured lifestyle, and, I thought, what would happen to me once I was discharged and walked back out into the real world without that structure? How could I do it alone? How could I cope with those who were in my life before rehab? Was I strong enough to take what I learned and use it without the safety net I had while in rehab? I could use the safety net as an excuse if I relapsed, or I could be accountable and responsible for myself. I chose to take responsibility for me and it worked. It was not easy, but it was do-able. I did it then and I do it today.

I had to make the choice whether or not to remove myself from my old lifestyle and friends who did not want to get better. It did not mean they were bad people or could not change. It meant that, at that time, they had lifestyles different from what I needed and wanted. It was OK. I also had to know my limits and set boundaries in situations and places I found myself in once I left rehab. By being aware and honest, I avoided the pitfalls that could have triggered a relapse. I don't test myself with people and situations that may trigger a need to numb myself with food, sex, or any of the other dysfunctional choices I made in my past. My choices make me who I am today. It's funny – I learned that we all have the potential to be and do anything we want in life, but potential alone does not make us who we are. It is the choices we make that define us.

My last stay in rehab taught me two things which have come to be the cornerstone of my recovery process and that I look at everyday. First is that I can not do it alone. I need others' help to get through the pain and suffering that I had thought no one could help me with. Second, I have choices, positive and negative. It is up to me to choose what is best. I was able to see that the choices I made in the past were not healthy or positive for me. If I was to change, then I needed to make positive choices on which I could build. No one could make those choices for me then and no one does it for me now.

The answers I knew in the past just kept me wallowing in my abyss until I summoned up enough courage and trust to ask others for guidance and help. The people who helped me did not give me answers – those I found within myself, as we all must. We just need a little guidance to show us the way. It was a very harrowing experience when I first asked for help and meant it, not like so many times I asked for help to maintain my dysfunctional lifestyle. I used to think when I asked for help it was a sign of weakness, but I now know it is a sign of strength. I learned that, together with others, I learn – alone, I struggle. Weakness does not exist in addicts like me or people like me with problems. We are vulnerable, but never have we been weak. We are afraid, rather than cowards as so many people think, lonely and scared rather than arrogant and rude. I know this to be true because for so long I could not share my pain with anyone, and the aloofness others perceived in me was a mask to cover my pain and self loathing.

When we go into rehab, one of the first thoughts we have, within the first minute, is *when can we get out?* How long will we have to deal with these people who do not know shit about us? I prayed each time I went into rehab that it would be over real soon. I plotted ways to escape or get thrown out, very dramatic on my part. But I was scared. When the day came for me to leave in 1994, I wanted to stay longer. I was just getting the hang of things and really getting to know *me*. I was scared that day, but excited to use what I learned to make the real world a place I could survive.

The build up the week before my discharge day was intense, with fear, anxiety, frustration, self-doubt, and wondering – could I really use the tools I had learned? How could I survive after being in rehab for so long?

Could I find a job? Where was I to live? With all the worry, I started to revert to my old ways to survive. I thought I could use new tools and combine them with old ways. It never works that way.

On discharge, I had few options. One was to go back to Sacramento with my family and away from the aftercare I could receive near the rehab. The second option was to find short term solutions to housing and getting a job to stay on track for my recovery. I chose number two, and it was not all that good for me. Even though I had great boundaries, at times I easily slipped into my manipulation and victimization of others. Now I say it like this because it was part "old me" and part "new me" trying to survive.

It was so easy to abide by the rules and regulations while in rehab because there was structure. The true test for me was the day I walked out of rehab. That day was the day that started my recovery. Now, I did not have the therapists to answer questions each day. Now, I did not have someone to cook my meals and talk to me about my fear of weight gain. Now, I did not have someone to help me through my nightmares. Now, I did not have someone to stop me from cutting myself or throwing myself into walls when the emotional pain overcame me. Now, I did not have the support from other patients. I felt alone and scared. I knew I had learned a lot, and had made progress, and that it was up to me. I did not expect perfection immediately when I walked out the doors of the rehab. What I knew was that I would have good and bad days and that I had the tools to deal with life in a whole new way. It was up to me now. I truly was in control, but for the first time in a healthy manner with support I had never known before. It was a whole new world and one I had to adapt to and live in. My world from the past was no longer a viable option.

It was very hard, but I was able to stay with a former patient who had been in rehab with me. She was a wonderful and loving lady who really was an inspiration to me. She lived real close to the rehab, so I could go to aftercare groups. She agreed to let me stay with her while I looked for a job and my own place. After a short time looking for jobs in restaurants, driving, and delivery, I was frustrated and exhausted. So I did what I knew best: I turned to my past to help me survive. I made a few phone calls and was able to connect with someone in my past who set me up to make quick money – for sex. Again, I was doing things sexually for large amounts of money. I justified it by telling myself I could make big money for a few encounters here and there. I secured a few new clients and one old one, who kept me floating in cash until I could find a job that paid me as much. Unfortunately, finding a job that paid that much was very hard to do. Why work hard, when I could make great money twice a week for just a few hours doing something I loved: Sex.

I knew what I was doing, and that this went against my recovery program, but at least I did not retreat to binging and purging to deal with the shame of sex for money as I had in the past. It was some small progress. This was a quick fix for a short period of time, I told myself. This lasted for about five months. Again I fooled myself into believing it would only be until I could get a real job. But the money was too good and too easy.

I could have gone back to Sacramento, but I knew that it was not a healthy place for me to live at this time. I had so many bad memories, and had hurt so many people there.

I did not want to be around them and start back where I was before rehab. I wanted to get back on my feet with a job and an apartment and a great recovery program before I went home. So many people thought I would not make it, and I did not want to prove them right. I wanted to show them the progress I had made after my stay in rehab – and since it was not forward progress, I decided to stay in Los Angeles rather than be riddled with shame and guilt around family and friends back home.

As I stayed in L.A., I continued to go back and forth between old coping behaviors and the tools I learned in rehab. I took steps forward and backward but I never gave up on me.

Once I was able to save some money, I moved out to my own apartment not far from the woman who had let me share her apartment. I used my ability to manipulate to bullshit the property manager into letting me move in without any money down and for three months before I paid a dime. It felt good to get this over on him, and at the same time I knew I was wrong. I dealt with the guilt each day, but allowed myself to think that I would right this wrong after I was able to survive with a new job. About this time, another former patient lent me money to help with the down payment for the apartment, and I blew it on everything else other than rent. I owe many people money from the past and one day I will repay it. I lied to everyone who was within earshot because I was still afraid to grow up and take care of myself without having someone do it for me. I went from family to friends to strangers to satisfy my need for survival and I victimized them again.

One thing I did was to be honest with myself more and more each day. It may seem as if I did not grow, but I was growing each day no matter what survival skills I had to use to take care of myself. Once I moved into this new apartment, I was alone with myself for the first time in my life – without a lifeline for support. This is when it all started to change for the better. I had been out ten months and really started to use the tools I had learned to make the changes I wanted but was so afraid to make. I was growing up and afraid and happy at the same time.

Living alone was and is still very scary for me. It is at these times that so many memories from the past come up. They can bury me to the point where I start thinking of the old ways to numb the pain. Once I moved into my own apartment, I realized that this was the real deal. I was going to either move through the past or let it consume me again out of fear and loneliness. I had been in a safe, secure place for almost 60 days, and then went from there to stay with someone. So, I had little time to be alone. My co-dependency issues were being met as long as I was around others. Being alone meant I had to depend on myself, and that was something I had never really done – to be accountable and responsible for *me* without having someone there to hold me. So, instead of having someone live with me I started a relationship based on pure sex and mutual loneliness.

During my time with her I was really able to see *me*, and that was hard to deal with. I did not go back to using food as medicine, even though I wanted to. I stayed clear from relapses of binging and purging. I got back into sex as the way to deal with everything. Even though we were two fucked-up people spending time together instead of helping ourselves, I was able to stay focused with the food issues and recovery. We had no real need for each other, except to stay focused on each other rather than on recovery. The sex was great, but that was it. Nothing else was compatible between us. I wanted to save her from the hell she lived in, and at the same time feel OK about my life. Wrong way to take care of me.

I realized that sex issues were very difficult to deal with. Sex was and is such a great relief and has always been so easy for me that it was like breathing, and I saw that I was transferring addictions to some degree. I could see my foundation being built one stone at a time. I was making progress, but slowly – and that was good for me. All the urges just to forget everything I learned in rehab and go with what felt best kept me up each night, but I was not going to let those urges defeat me again.

This so-called great relationship ended when I helped her move to Aspen, Colorado. I met her ex-boyfriend in Malibu and packed up a cargo trailer to take what she needed to get away from California. I realized as I was doing this – and getting paid by him – that I was not doing anything here that was good for me. I learned when I went to his house that they were still together. He had no idea who I was other than a former patient in the same rehab she had been in, and that she was doing me a favor by getting me this work. I needed the money but not the hell I was going to face now that I knew the truth. When I confronted her with this new information, she told me he was still in the picture. It was not like we would be together, but I did not want someone stalking me because I was with his girlfriend. I delivered everything to Aspen and stayed for a few days. All the drama I went through made it easier for me to see that my recovery was the most important thing I could do, and that I needed to make choices that were positive and healthy for me. I decided to leave my past in the past and really work on *me*. I did not want people like her in my life, and I did not want to be who I had been in the past. I had to get away from where I was living in L.A. and start anew. That journey began the day I returned to L.A. from Aspen.

Back in L.A., I knew that it would be very difficult to make it on my own. I could not really keep up the charade to myself that I was OK and able to do it my way. I could not keep going forward then backwards. I was tired and needed to get away from everything and everyone, so I made a phone call to a dear friend in Riverside, California. I called my friend Mike and his wife Alice, and asked if I could stay with them for awhile until I could get back on my feet. I was in the middle of nowhere but safe from myself and my past for the time being.

I got a job at The Riverside Press selling subscriptions. It was fun for a while, and I was the top salesperson from the first week until I quit. I would work the night shift, and always wanted to come up with excuses to not go to work – but I did go. I fought myself constantly because I hated working for someone other than myself. They set the rules and I actually kept up with them.

This was the first time I could remember in a long, long time that I had a legit job working for someone else. I was enjoying everything about staying in Riverside and working. It felt good to take care of *me* and be in a place that was not challenging me to go back to old habits.

Mike and Alice were two of the angels in my life over the years. I will always cherish my friendship with them and love them for the people they are. I know we would be there for each other in a heartbeat.

I was getting lonely and bored working and just going home each night. I was starting to feel trapped and wanted to get back to L.A. I wore out my welcome when Mike and I had a difference of opinion on how I should live my life. I had a problem with people telling me how to live when they needed to take care of their own lives before trying to control mine. I was not binging or purging, or acting out with food or sex, I just wanted to make a change. I decided to leave Riverside and head back to L.A.

Back in Los Angeles, I had to decide to keep working the process I had discovered or keep lying to myself. I chose to take the next year to work on myself and build a solid foundation. I did this with the help of family and friends who really cared and were able to see that I was trying. I realized that I could have the great life that I was meant to have, without going back to my old lifestyle for answers. I am always aware of my past, because for me to stay strong and healthy I have to keep healthy boundaries, and because as an addict there is always a chance I could go back to the lifestyle I worked so hard to escape. I do not lie and tell myself all is picture perfect. I tell myself each day that I have a wonderful opportunity to make a difference for me and for others. And I do. Since I started my recovery process, so many great things have happened and are happening each day of my life. The reason they are happening is because I took responsibility for who and what I am in life, good and bad.

One thing that has allowed me to get to the serenity I have in my life today is that I have no regrets. Sure, I did many things to others and myself and have made amends to the best of my ability. It may sound harsh that I have no regrets, but I have learned that if I keep regretting what I did in my past, I will never have a future filled with happiness and joy. The past is not something I can ever un-do – nor do I want to. I know that I hurt people, and have done the best I can with what I have to ask for their forgiveness. Some people will never forgive me; that is not in my control. I learned a long time ago that, in order for me to move on to today and tomorrow, I have to be OK with my past. If we continue to let our pasts control and lead us, we can never make changes. The past has taught us, and I have learned so many valuable lessons from the person I used to be. I thank God for who I was then and who I am now. One without the other would not complete my journey.

Today I live each day with the hope that I can face anything life deals me and get through it, without regressing to past emotional medicine such as abusing food or sex, lying or gambling or manipulating others for my personal needs. I get through each day knowing that *I* did it – no one else. By doing it myself, I have built the self-esteem and courage to face many obstacles that I had created or that others created in front of me. By believing in myself and what I can do, I will never need my past dysfunctional medicines to help me love myself or to make me feel good about who and what I am.

In the past, I played the victim *so* well. That allowed me to stay in my dysfunctional lifestyle, because I knew how to push everyone's and anyone's emotional buttons so they would feel sorry for me and take care of me. I made victims of so many people – family, friends, loved ones, strangers – but *I* was never a victim. By accepting that and knowing it to be the truth, I saw that by playing the victim I was allowing myself to live with my addictions in my distorted world. I was my own worst enemy, and at times I still am. That is OK now, because *I* control my future – not food, sex, gambling, lying, *et cetera*. I take the credit for the good things I do and responsibility for my mistakes.

Each day I take an inventory of what I have to do for me, personally, in order to feel good about myself and the choices I make. I understand that each choice has negative and positive consequences for which I am responsible. The choices I make today represent the person I have become on my journey. I feel great each time a make a choice based on good information and the understanding that *I* am responsible and no one else. I no longer blame anyone or anything else for my life. It is mine and mine alone with God. If my choices do not work as I had hoped, I find another way to make things happen. I do not revert to self-abuse or numbing substances as I did in the past. It feels great. It used to be so hard to even think about these things, so I just made continuous negative choices. Now the choices I make are positive and healthy for me both mentally and physically. I no longer tell myself it is OK to start tomorrow. I had years and years of starting tomorrow. I do what I need to do each day for me to feel good and to be responsible and accountable for myself. I also know that what I do not get done today does not mean that I have failed, it means I have tomorrow to finish it or the next day. I no longer set goals that I know I cannot keep, to make it easier to give up. I set realistic boundaries for work, people, friends, family, and career. This makes it easier for me to get things done, one project at a time. I have learned to let people into my life and trust them to help me, rather than to try to do everything alone and fail.

In my recovery process I have learned what I really need to know about *me* as a person, and it is not always easy to accept things about ourselves.

I remember one thing that really hurt as a child. It was always on Valentine's Day when I was at Holy Cross grade school. Each year I got the fewest cards from girls and they let me know it. The kids would make fun of me and it killed me inside. I learned to let things that bothered me go deep inside and fester. There are things I face today that bother me in the same way, but I do not let them sit and fester. I have chosen to talk with people who I trust and respect on a personal level, and who are willing to listen and give me feedback. At times, I face situations that bring back horrible memories and I sit stunned for a moment. I collect my thoughts and look at my options and see the solutions very clearly. As a youngster, I did not know options that would help me.

I could go on, but what I am trying to tell you is that there were no instant miracles that allowed me to be cured overnight. Recovery is a process. It takes time to get the positive results we seek. I faced my past and overcame my old habits and behaviors to get to where I am today. Through hard work, honesty, and many tears, I built the solid foundation I have today and share with many people.

In September of 1997, I began building on the foundation I made for my own recovery, in order to share it with others who are willing to take chances and make changes. It took me three years to build my recovery process after my discharge in 1994. I had to find answers and solutions to problems in my life on my own, without relying on or looking to someone else to give them to me or do things for me. I became accountable and responsible for me. During those 3 years, I monitored my up and down moments and emotions to better use my new coping skills. I learned to keep moving forward, even though I would have different degrees of setbacks to overcome. And overcome them I do, by being honest in that one moment I have to make a decision – a decision to either deal with the situation or return to my old dysfunctional coping skills. Even though there is a strong pull to choose my past behaviors, I know what will happen if I choose my past. Today, I choose to go forward.

Chapter Fifteen: From There To Here

How did I get from the person you met in the beginning to the person I am today? You have read about my trials and tribulations, how I wanted so bad at times to get through my days without hurting myself or others but was not able to. Some of my actions were unexplainable – I did not really know why I did some of the things I did to soothe my pain. Later, after working on myself and learning more, I was able to understand. What you are about to read explains what worked for me to get me to the place I am now from the life you have read about so far. From the days of binging and purging and selling myself for enough money to eat and pay bills, this is what saved my life. Nothing comes easy or overnight. The process I went through is different from yours or anyone else's. On the road to and through recovery of any kind, what we have in common is the desire to live a healthy and nurturing life. This is a realistic goal.

Even though I had to work hard to get to where I am in life today, there are many times when I miss the friends who stood by me and held my hand during those dark and scary nights: My friends Ronald, Jack, Carl, Mr. King, and Wendy. I miss their warmth, their caring, their love, and their answers to my problems. They were never the bad guys. I just used them as I did others to make myself feel better. I victimized them for what they could give me to numb myself. How many can say that McDonald's, Jack in The Box, Carl's Jr., Burger King, and Wendy's herself were real friends? In my world, they were. Today I do not need them or any of the other coping strategies I fabricated that kept me from growing as a person and living a life full of joy and happiness and self-respect and love.

To lead the healthy and productive life I have now, I had to learn through trial and error to forgive myself for the person I used to be and the person I always thought I was. I had to be honest with myself. That released my ability to learn and to see things from a different perspective than I had while in my eating disorder and self destructive mode. I learned that forgiveness of self is the window to recovery. Forgiving myself is not a "get out of jail free" card for what I had done to myself and others. I earned my own forgiveness by recognizing and acknowledging the consequences of my actions, thoughts, and behaviors. I have never nor will I ever erase my past. I take full responsibility for what I did and who I was. Learning to forgive myself was the single hardest part of my recovery process, because I felt at times that forgiving myself meant I was just avoiding my responsibilities toward the past. I did not let them go. I embraced them and made them part of my present life, to address when the time was right and then handle in the best way I knew. I learned through self-forgiveness that I could not change others' opinions and ideas about me, and that what they felt was what they needed to feel. My job is not to change others but myself. And I have.

Forgiveness is the one thing I hear so many people ask of others because of something they did or said, and I did this in the past. I thought that if you forgave me then my negative behaviors and actions – my sins - were absolved. I then realized that I also forgave people for the abuse and horror I lived through to reach this moment in my life. I realized that forgiving others was not something that made my life better. People did and said what they did for many reasons that had nothing to do with me, but I was in the way. The only true healing power I have – and it is a gift we all share – is to forgive myself. Point 10 in *The Daily Process, 16 Points to Life*© says, "I've forgiven myself for what I appeared to be." That is how my mind cleared to start my road to and through recovery. With this forgiveness came being honest with myself about who I was, who I am, and who I want to be. Those nights and days of hating myself for eating too much, binging, looking in the mirror, lying, stealing, prostituting myself, manipulating and victimizing others are over, because I have learned to love myself and accept myself for the good things I have to offer in life and the bad things I have done to survive in my world-as-it-was-before.

In the next chapter you will read about what I learned on my journey to find the real person behind my eating disorder, sex addiction, and other issues I faced in life, and how I handle life today. The one constant is *the person you first met in the beginning of this book is the same person you are reading about now*. The only difference is I deal with the reality of who I am rather than numb myself with outside "medicine" (food, sex, stealing, lying, *et cetera*). I am no longer ashamed of myself, and I love myself more than I could ever have thought possible. It may seem self-indulgent, but without my self-love you would not be reading this book and I would not be here.

In order to forgive myself, I really had to look at my life in order to understand the difference between what was real and what I perceived to be real because of my paranoia, depression, anxiety, and self-hate. I know from experience that if I told myself I was a loser or bad person, for example because I could not go through a day without binging or purging, then I believed I was worthless because I could not carry out this simple task. This self-hate did not let me see the truth behind my inability to be productive. I interpreted it as bad or degrading and hurt myself more. In my mind, I deserved all the negative things I went through in life, because I could not change. But I did not have the tools then, and the self-hate was so strong that self-forgiveness was something I could not even imagine.

I always looked at my role in any situation from a perspective of fear or self-hatred or both. With these two factors leading the way, I was not able to see how I might have acted or responded to situations in ways that might have helped turn the tide in my life *then*. If I sensed anyone trying to change me I would rebel, because I knew they had no idea what I was going through. How could they help? How could someone without my lifestyle, experience, and past know what it was like to wake up everyday being me? So, it was easy to shut them out, enabling me to stay in that warm blanket of dysfunction.

Being a people pleaser and oh, so needy, I wanted others to like and accept me for the person I was, even though I didn't know who I was myself. This way of living kept me from getting to know the real me and what I was capable of accomplishing in my life. I wanted to be liked so much that I did many things I did not really want to do. I did not want to be alone. Being alone was very depressing and sad.

To combat these feelings, I created *The Daily Process, 16 Points to Life*© when I was in my last rehabilitation facility in 1994. (See page 172.) Since I did not really understand or care for the 12-step programs at that time, I knew I had to have something that allowed me to get through each day and help me overcome my fear and self-hatred. These *Points* were also the groundwork for THE NUTRITION & BODY IMAGE PROGRAM™ I wrote for myself in 1997. This program is not just for those of us who deal with eating disorders or addiction. It allows anyone to make changes they desire for the better life they seek. It just so happens I am a man with an eating disorder and this program changed my life.

While researching and looking for the help I needed, I realized that I had no connection between my mind and my body, no concept of what they needed to be healthy together. My mind and body played tricks on me when it came to food, fear, anxiety, sex, and self-esteem. I sought to find a way that would allow a healthier lifestyle based upon respect for the needs of both my mind and my body. That is how THE NUTRITION & BODY IMAGE PROGRAM™ came about. By understanding this connection I have learned that being responsible for how I treat myself allows me to function both mentally and physically in a healthy manner, something I had not really known until I began my process to recovery.

Since my main problem was my eating disorder, I set out to learn the negative and positive effects that food and exercise had on me. I looked at why I used food, blamed food, hated my body, hated my face, and so forth. I wanted to know why I felt these urges to hurt myself using food. The PROGRAM allowed me to look at what was real and to be honest to myself about what changes I could make that would be positive for me, rather than enabling my self-abuse – using food to cure any and all emotional and physical pain and discomfort. By thinking that less of me –

meaning less weight, smaller waist, gaunt face, smaller pants size, *et cetera* – was always best, I knew in my distorted world that I would be fine if I achieved "less". The media were not to blame. So many people need to find fault elsewhere rather than look for the truth in themselves. If we continue to blame others, we will never find the answers we seek. Blame takes the focus off of self and makes someone else responsible. For me to blame others for everything just kept me emotionally crippled.

We are not all alike. We have many things in common, but one thing that makes us different is our respective abilities and desires to change. Now, I know that change is not easy and can bring more pain than pleasure. But I know through my own life that change is possible and right in front of us – if we really want it. The big word here is "if." For so many years I knew what would happen if I changed how I lived, but I was afraid to do the little things needed to change my life, let alone the big things. I saw how others lived and dealt with issues, far differently from the way I did, and it seemed to work for them. But my eating disorder and addictions served a purpose for me then: They were my identity. If I gave them up, who would I be, to me and to others? What would I be? How could I cope? Hard questions at the time, but through THE NUTRITION & BODY IMAGE PROGRAM™ the answers became clear and easy to see. My knowledge of my needs was very limited. What I needed each day was a fix for my pain and nothing and nobody was going to stop me, even my own death. The Program showed me that I can have personal success in my life – and still be part of society as an individual – without turning to the self-medication methods of my past.

By following the Program, I have gained the knowledge I sought for so many years – why I did the things I did to myself and others to cope with the problems I faced in life. I now know why I turned to food, sex, stealing, prostitution, victimizing others, and all my other dysfunctional thoughts, actions, and behaviors – why I needed that lifestyle to live and cope in a world I helped create.

As a member of this society, doing what so many people did and still do, I looked for the answers to all my problems in short-term solutions, solutions that never lasted more than a day, a "quick fix" mentality. I blamed everyone and everything for my problems – except myself, of course. I wanted to be cured from my eating disorder and life's unjust torture without ever really looking at the emotional and physical consequences. I knew pain would come after I created and carried out a destructive act upon myself or others, but I was so used to it that I would just say "fuck it" to myself. I would hope and pray that there was some chance, however small, that I could make the changes needed to stop these behaviors and actions.

This did not and will not work for me or you. No matter how convinced we are that it is the right choice, the outcome proved the same every time for me – and will for you as well: Pain, depression, self-hate, and so much more. I was always able to get what I *wanted*, but I never, ever got what I *needed* to be healthy or productive from any of these behaviors, thoughts, or actions. They were temporary solutions to problems I did not know otherwise how to address.

THE NUTRITION & BODY IMAGE PROGRAM™ has given me a better understanding of what my mind and body need to work together to operate at their full potential for the betterment of my life. And today, the mind-body connection I have allows me to look at myself as a person and human being who has needs in life that can be fulfilled – if I continue to make the changes I need for the healthy foundation I build on each day. I make those changes when they are needed, not for others but for myself.

So many people use the word "diet" as pertaining to limiting food intake and weight loss. I understand that, and see where people might think a particular diet is for them because it supposedly worked for others. But "diet" stands for "**d**angerous **i**dentity-**e**nhancing **t**rap". When we diet, we are setting ourselves up for negative results. A diet to me is a form of self-punishment for doing something we may have enjoyed but are doing a little too much – something we all have done or will do in life at some time – or we diet to gain attention or affection. What a diet does is keep us trying to make changes that are quick and easy – a quick solution – without looking at the consequences down the line. I lived this "diet" for years. I thought if I did things a certain way I would get the results I sought *now*, but I learned through THE NUTRITION & BODY IMAGE PROGRAM™ that the results I need in life take time, and that once I get them the time spent is well worth it.

My "pride" (**p**redictable **r**esponse **i**n **d**efensive **e**nvironments) was a precursor to many of my problems. I had all the answers and knew everything, therefore no one could help me or tell me what to do. I had so much pride that I could not accept – as many people cannot – that I needed help to get better. I needed others to help me get to the point that I could do it for myself. This foolish pride almost killed me on more than one occasion.

THE NUTRITION & BODY IMAGE PROGRAM™ is the guide I used to find the path that led me to the solid foundation I build upon each day. The *16 Points* allowed me to look at myself clearly and honestly, leading to me being able to forgive myself with a clear conscience. Since the one thing I really lacked during my destructive days was responsibility to myself, others, and society, these *Points* guided me to take responsibility for my thoughts, actions, and behaviors as well as become accountable for everything I did and will do. By grasping these *Points*, I was able to provide myself with the nurturing I had always sought from food, sex, gambling, and all my other dysfunctional behaviors. *I* was the main focus in each Point – not God, friends, family, or society. By knowing that it was OK to make choices, fall on my face and get back up, question God, take ten steps forward and eight steps back no matter the outcome, I could use these *Points* as the foundation for my recovery process. They have been that foundation since the first day I used them.

Each Point represents growth in my life as a person, and has allowed me to forgive myself and look at what I did in the past without self-hate or self-abuse. I have a choice: If I want to let my past control me, I can. But, like you, I want a better today and an even better tomorrow. I am not saying every day is perfect, but I can turn a bad day into a healthy, productive day because I am now honest with myself and use the *16 Points* as a guide. Following the path I have set for myself now brings many opportunities that I had never been able to see or grasp. These "new" opportunities have always been there, but I had never been able to see them. We tend to grasp the first thing we see as the answer without really looking at it for negative consequences. With the *16 Points*, I have learned to ask myself and others questions without fear. They lead me on my search for the truth about myself and my life, help build up the strengths I have inside my heart and mind, let me take responsibility no matter the consequences, allow me to become accountable for myself to myself, and nurture and heal my mind, body, and spirit.

These *16 Points* have also taught me courage, self-confidence, self-limitations, how to deal with fear of failure, boundaries, self-awareness, faith, honesty, my identity, and self-healing. The *16 Points* rely heavily on spiritual belief. It is not a belief in any one religion or faith, but a belief that there is a power or spirit or guide out there for each of us, and that to become aware of that power is to gain an ally – the strength to tackle each day as it comes. The *16 Points* have led me to be a stronger person and feel more alive than I have ever in my past. They were the impetus to start my journey to recovery.

By using THE NUTRITION & BODY IMAGE PROGRAM™ as a guide, I have learned to understand the choices I made in my past and what purposes they served, and to replace them with positive and healthy choices. I have mentioned many moments of self destruction. Each of those moments I have learned from. They have come full circle under this Program.

I tried to get to recovery through the help and guidance of others (rehabilitation centers, doctors, *et cetera*). They did what they could, but they never made the difference I have made in my own life. I knew that I had to make it OK to deal with my past self-destructive habits and that those habits had to cease if I was to go on and make the changes that allow me to fall on my face without going back to past coping skills and habits as solutions. I needed to know it was safe to open up about myself, be honest, and forgive myself without my past demons waiting to smother me with self-abuse and self-hate.

One issue that many of us suffer from is the need to *control*. Mine was huge, but in order to get to a healthy lifestyle that allowed me to grow as a person, I needed to understand that I had to control that need to control.

Now I am clear about one thing that allows me to wake up every morning loving myself more and more each day: I have come to learn and realize that my past choices were never *wrong*, they were the only choices I had for the coping skills I knew, and they just did not work for me. The three main struggles I had during my active eating disorder days were with food, body image, and self-esteem. I thought in black and white. In my distorted world there was no grey, so when I made a slight mistake I would just dive head first into self-abuse. My thinking was that if I could not do it right – *my* way of right – then I might as well just abuse myself until I could get my thoughts straight on how to approach the next day with a healthy outline. I was not able to put one and one together and see the self-destruction in which I engaged each day. I was living like Bill Murray's character in "Groundhog Day" (a movie in which each day was the same day as the one before, the same thing over and over and over), but I knew no way of stopping. However, with the Program I was able to connect the elements that led me to past behaviors, and to change my need for self-medication by looking at each situation head on and dealing with it as it arose.

What I was able to see is that I could no longer use food, gambling, sex, relationships, or compulsive lying as substitutes for feelings. My feelings are genuine and real and *mine*. It is OK for me to feel and OK for me to work through my feelings toward a healthy solution. I do not have to drug myself in order to feel or to *not* feel. My "medicine" never allowed me to feel. It suppressed my feelings so I could hide from reality. I understand now that my black and white thinking would only lead to continued self-abuse. It was not the solution to any of the issues I faced then and can face today. These periods of despair filled a 24-hour day. My fear of change kept me feeding my habits. I kept denying to myself that I needed help, so it was easy to stay distracted from reality. The dysfunctional thoughts, behaviors, and actions I lived out were tremendous burdens. THE NUTRITION & BODY IMAGE PROGRAM™ is the guide by which I have been able to put healthy balance into my life surrounding, work, family, health, recreation, relationships, sex, food, exercise, and so much more.

The one struggle I always thought was my main problem from the beginning of my eating disorder were my problems with food. I did not know until later that I used food as a drug to assuage my emotional pain, and when it did not work I used the other dysfunctional activities in my life. My paranoia – as to what was too much, my trigger foods, how foods made me feel physically and emotionally, emotional eating binges, eating out of anger and self-hate, and all the reasons I would eat other than that I needed fuel for my mind and body to survive – is gone now. It is funny that until years into my recovery process I never really looked at food as pure enjoyment. Don't get me wrong – I *llllloooovvvveeeedddd* food for what I used it for, a drug. As I eat now, I can taste food, feel its texture, smell it, have no fear of it, take my time at a meal, leave food on my plate, eat foods that I have not prepared, eat at different restaurants, eat at different times of the day, not hoard food or hide it in bathrooms before going out to dinner. Food is nurturing to me because I allow it to be and deal with the underlying issues that drove me to use food as medicine in my past. I have learned to feel this way toward food because it is a simple way of addressing food.

All this great awareness came from me looking at five simple words that helped me separate my food intake from my emotional needs. These five simple words I now use with my food plan (or program or whatever you want to call it – I prefer "way of life") are *why, what, when, where,* and *how* I eat today. This sounds very simple – almost too simple – but when dealing with an eating disorder, disordered eating, or emotional eating, these five words make a difference. They make a difference because I have made changes in how I approach each of these words in relationship to my eating habits.

One word here that has been very important throughout my recovery is *change*. Winston Churchill said, "To improve is to change; to be perfect is to change often." Great words of wisdom. In my past, I wanted everything perfect so that I could overcome this silent killer, my eating disorder. But I never made any changes in my thoughts, actions, or behaviors so that "perfection" could become a reality on an daily and continuous basis.

Today "perfection" means to me that I am constantly striving to better myself, as a person and as a member of society, by making those changes that allow me to overcome unhealthy lifestyle coping skills from my past. When I face an issue (depression, anxiety, fear, loneliness, *et cetera*) today, I look to what changes I can make to deal with these feelings in a healthy and nurturing way.

Chapter Sixteen: What I Learned

I want to share with you how I handle some issues now that my foundation is growing stronger and expanding each day due to the "*16 Points*" and "THE NUTRITION & BODY IMAGE PROGRAM™."

Change:

Today I am very fortunate to be able to look at situations, see my part in them, and make the changes needed to benefit my life. I no longer look at a situation and see only one option. I see numerous options because I have allowed myself the possibility that change can bring about happiness and success in my life and those around me. Sometimes it is not easy to try new ideas and make changes, but I also know that by allowing change to be an opportunity I have a win-win situation. By opening myself up to change I have had many new experiences that I never knew I could have. I recognize that it is never too late in life to become what I might have been, and without trying I never would have got to where I am today. I know it is time in my life to pass from one phase to another with new hope and challenges that I can endure.

Before, I was resistant to change because change meant I had to put aside the lifestyle I led – the only one I really knew. My lifestyle was my safety net for all the pain I endured. That lifestyle kept me from growing as a person in any aspect of my life. When I finally decided to change things in my life, it was scary, nerve wracking, lonely, and, most of all, I did not know if I had the ability to change. Who I was and how I lived my life kept me in an emotionally safe place like my mom's womb. It was warm, isolated, and I really had to do nothing. As in the womb, I had others feeding my lifestyle and allowing me my comforts without consequences to me.

I have seen the changes in history from one civilization to another, and how earlier civilizations have all but vanished but still have a positive effect on our society today. Without change we would not have new medicines, health care, our environment would be depleted, no new technology, no new religions, and we would not be the free world. Change in my life has brought about actions which in turn have led me to new discoveries. I needed to grow as a person, and change has allowed me that positive and nurturing growth that was stunted with my past thoughts and behaviors. By allowing change into my life, it has brought about new peace of mind for me, self-respect, communication skills, self-love, calmness, faith, brought me closer to those I love and who love me, success, and the ability to share what I have learned with others from a positive and healthy point of view. Change is inevitable – it is just its timing that can be tricky.

Co-dependency:

Today I no longer look for others to fill the void I had from the experiences I had endured. I realized that my co-dependency tendencies were a way to cope with traumatic events in my past or situations I could not handle. Often I needed to have someone else to turn to, to relieve any pain I was suffering, because I could not do it alone. I realized that when I was co-dependent I turned to people who were not healthy for me. I realized, as I worked on myself through recovery, that I had a better chance of finding solutions to my problems if I took control and faced my needs with honesty and determination. I work on and face issues today that in the past would have led me to need someone to make it better. *I* make it better now.

Family:

The people I loved the most are the ones I hurt the most, because I knew they would always be there – why I did not know. What I do know is that a family is a wonderful thing to have if you are lucky enough to have one. I was lucky then and still am. When it comes to my family, I had to realize that they had their own issues, brought on by circumstances that had nothing to do with me. How they dealt with them I could not control. And because I dealt with my issues concerning family, it did not mean I betrayed them. Sometimes, in the past, I felt I was telling secrets about my family, and that other people would look at them in a bad light. Well, the truth is the truth, and in order for me to survive I had to deal with my family issues.

Today, I accept responsibility for my part in anything that hurt my family, and realize that was then, this is now. Some things they chose to not let go of, and that is OK for them – they need to hold on for some reason. I chose to let the past go and live for today. I have boundaries with my family that allow for as healthy a relationship as I can have with them. I do not give power or control to them, because this is *my* life, not theirs. I am responsible for me, not my family anymore. And the reason they stayed there with me when I hurt them was they loved me unconditionally.

Media:

The media and its influence on society has never been the reason for my eating disorder or other dysfunctional behaviors. The media has but one job to do and that is to sell you and I on their opinions, ideas, clothes, travel, exercise workouts, etc. To me when we give control to the media by saying they are the reason eating disorders exist, then we are blaming someone or something rather than looking for the real reasons behind why anyone suffers from an eating disorder. Anything can influence our thoughts, but we are the ones who choose food – or any other substance or behavior – to cure the pain we suffer.

Binge/Purge:

Today I have no need to binge and purge my food for emotional relief. In the past the purging was a way of getting rid of the disgust I had for myself because I could not control myself and needed to cleanse what I thought were impurities from my body, meaning the food and negative thoughts I had about myself. It is funny. The binging made me feel good at that moment and allowed me to numb myself, then the purge would hurt like hell from the constant vomiting, exercise, and laxatives. I know that the binging and purging filled a need for comfort, and I thought it was comfort for my lack of control. The only way I was able to stop the binging and purging was to take it one day at a time. I could not stop cold turkey, and I learned it was OK to slowly wean myself down from binging and purging ten times a day to the day I stopped completely. It took me almost four months.

Body Image:

Today I love my body and the way it looks and feels. I no longer use a mirror as a measuring stick as to how my body looks, setting the tone for my day. With an eating disorder, the distorted belief that my body had to look a certain way in order for each day to be productive was crazy and dysfunctional to the max. I am sure some of you can relate. At a time when I was using so many negative coping skills to deal with my self-hatred, every time I would look at any part of my body, I would hate myself even more because I felt that my body was my identity. The underlying issues that I could not grasp led me to look at my body and say to myself, "I can control how it looks no matter what I have to do." And control it I did, because it was right there in front of me. The only coping skills I had with a body I hated were to starve it, stuff it, cut it, punch it, and abuse it any way I could to get it to feel and look as I needed it to look, in order to feel good about myself and be accepted by others. I thought I *had* to be accepted by others. I have since learned I do not need others' validation. If I hated me then you hated me as well. If I had a day, and there were maybe two days in my past when I thought that my body looked good to me in the mirror game, then I would treat it nice. Good food, exercise, and rest. But what I saw 99.9% of the time, in mirrors, car windows, anything with a reflection, was shameful and disgusting.

As time went on and I learned more about myself and my eating disorder, I realized that my body was not the cause or answer to the problems I had that led me to use food as medicine for the pain I endured.

I worked to overcome my body image issues by accepting that it was under *my* control – not food or the need to be accepted for what I looked like by others. I could find the solutions to the problems that led me to abuse myself with food. I realized that after all the self-abuse my body was damaged and worn out. How could it look as I wanted it to if I abused it and did not feed it or take care of it properly? I exercised too much some times and then not at all at others. I ate for hours some days and then did not eat for days at a time. Was this really loving myself or my body? No, it was not. If I was going to make changes, I needed to be healthier in my thoughts about body image. I had to have a different view of how my body looked other than the hateful view I had for so many years.

I began to accept that I needed to focus on the underlying issues that were the cause of my dysfunctional lifestyle and work to change my distorted thoughts and actions. Once I saw that my body was a temple to be loved and cherished, I began to let go of the negativity I had toward my appearance. I learned that I am different from others, and that my body responded to my abuse the best ways it knew how. I realized that it was going to take time to get over the body image issues I had, and that by making changes in my thought patterns toward my body I would succeed in dealing with this very difficult obsession.

I asked myself a simple question: What does my body have to do with my success in relationships, work, play, adventures, sex, and so forth? The correct answer is that as long as I was healthy, no matter what my body looked like I could have great success in whatever I did. It was up to me. So I looked at why in my distorted world I needed to look a certain way. The answer was I lacked self-esteem and love for myself as a person. Without these, it was easy to abuse my body and make it a focus of my life. Sure I could look great, but it was what was under the hood (my mind) that made me go. I overcame my body image issues by working on my inner self. I accepted that I am not perfect, that there is no such thing as "perfection" for me. I began to look at my body as a gift from God and, in order to enjoy it and use it for my benefit, I had to treat it with great respect and love. I nourish my body with massages, appropriate exercise, and proper food. I no longer starve it. I pamper my body, because if it goes I go. In all my paranoia about my body I have never had someone say anything negative about it, it was me and only me who saw something negative, and for years I suffered because I was blind. I love every inch of my body today. Sure there are some days when I say to myself I could look better, but that is natural. I have learned that my body is not who I am.

Fear of rejection:

Today I do not have the constant fear that other people will reject me because of the person I was in my past or who I am today. I always believed when I was in my dysfunctional lifestyle that others would not want anything to do with me. Because I had such self hatred, I thought they would hate me as well. My feeling of rejection came from my inability to love myself and treat myself with respect. If *I* rejected my needs and wants, then why would others not do the same?

Fear of abandonment:

Today I have no fear that someone will choose to end a friendship or relationship with me. I understand now that I am only part of that equation. I do not control why someone would want to leave or stop dealing with me. I accept my part without blame. I have gotten to the place in my life where I do not put my emotions, needs, or wants into another person's hands.

Loneliness:

Today I have no fear of being alone with myself. In the past, I was very lonely because I isolated myself from others, due to my need to find a cure for my pain and the dysfunctional behaviors, thoughts, and ideas that brought about that false sense of comfort. When I was alone, I craved to be with others who were like minded, which meant as dysfunctional as I was. My loneliness reinforced my use of food and other addictions as substitutes for people in my life. I am no longer a lonely man, because my own company is wonderful and the company I keep with others is balanced and healthy. I do not have to hide away to deal with my pain anymore. I chose in the past to isolate myself out of fear. Now I choose *not* to isolate myself, which brings change and great people into my life.

Denial:

Denial is a failure to accept the truth. In my past, I did not accept the truth about myself or my situations, and thought I could handle everything by turning to my dysfunctional lifestyle. Well, I was wrong. I do not live in denial today. I see the person I am and see everything around me with open eyes. I accept my responsibilities, so I *cannot* live in denial. I no longer run and hide from the obvious. I face it head on. I accept my strengths and weaknesses, and try to expand my strengths and strengthen my weaknesses. I have no need to return to old habits of denial for a sense of security or comfort. It no longer serves my needs.

Food:

My dear, dear friend, Food. Oh, how I love thee, let me count the ways. This is what I used to say often to myself when I chose food as the relief from all my pain in life. Food was just a numbing tool for the emotional trauma I endured each day – and the easiest drug to obtain. Today I do not see food or use food as I did in past. Since 1998, I have built a solid understanding of what food provides me in my life both emotionally and physically.

I learned to ask myself five simple questions about food, until they became imbedded in my memory and second nature. Why do I eat? What do I eat? Where do I eat? When do I eat? How do I eat? I know many people have asked these questions, but how many have really learned the truth behind each one? I have, for my own needs, to understand my life better, and take control over those times when I am tempted to use food as medicine instead of dealing with the issues I face in life.

Why do I eat? Because it is nourishment for my mind and body to work as one. I do not eat out of anger, depression, loneliness, fear, anxiety, or sadness anymore. Food is no longer my enemy or my medicine.

What do I eat? I eat anything I want. In the past I had so-called trigger foods. During emotional turmoil I would eat certain foods because they helped numb my pain. Food is no longer the numbing agent in my world. I eat all styles of food. I eat sweets, carbohydrates, breads, *et cetera*. But my eyes are not bigger than my stomach, if you know what I mean. I may eat more in one meal than another, but I do not cut back the next day to compensate for a larger meal. Not anymore. I eat what I want.

Where do I eat? I look at where I eat because it gives me a perspective of what is going on around me during a meal. I like to have time to eat meals without being rushed. There are times I am rushed, but I do not stuff food – I make time to eat it. If I can, you can. I make sure I do not eat in the car because it is like guzzling food. I do not eat while working because there is stress in work and I want my body to digest food. If I eat at a restaurant, I eat what I want and leave what I do not want – simple now, but not before. I look at the location where I eat meals to make sure all is calm, to enjoy the meal. And it works.

When do I eat? I look to eat my meals three times a day, with some small meals in between if I need them. I never miss breakfast, because it gives my body nourishment and keeps me from possibly overeating at lunch. I never eat late at night because it really serves no purpose for me. I like to go to bed at least five hours after my last meal. I eat when my body says it is hungry, and I have a great body clock now as to when I feel hungry.

How do I eat? This is a big one for me. I used to eat on the run, stuff myself real fast for next food item, binge, diet, finish others' meals, skip meals, hide food in the car and house, *et cetera*. Now, I eat peacefully no matter where my meals take place. I do not make meals stressful or have time limits as I did before. I can leave food now on a plate. Before I would think that was just wrong, kind of like dating a cousin.

Today I have no anxiety as I did in the past when it comes to planning meals. I know that I need to eat in order to have fuel for my mind and body. When I plan meals now

I eat different things because I like to try new foods. At restaurants I eat favorite foods at favorite restaurants. There are restaurants that prepare certain foods that taste better to me so I go there. I do not panic if my meal times are not met – I eat when I can.

This is the relationship I have with food today. Food is no longer my enemy, my identity, nor my best friend. When I am emotional, I know food is not the answer, so I do not turn to it. I turn to someone for help to deal with everything I turned to food for in the past. I do not panic around food anymore, nor, if I miss a meal, do I eat more the next meal. I have balance in my life and that allows for my food program to have balance as well.

Stress:

Today, I handle stressful situations with relative ease. I have learned to have patience with myself, with others, and with situations, which has led to much happiness in my life. I know now that there is only so much I can control, so I do not panic when I face situations that would have caused me to look to food or other dysfunctional behaviors to cope. In my past, stress made me feel like Gumby, being pushed and pinched in many directions at one time. Now, that weight has been lifted so I can seek solutions without added pressure. My mental well-being and physical well-being are no longer in jeopardy, because I have learned how to handle stress in any form or shape. I look at each situation or moment, see what my involvement is, and go from there. I do not take on more than I can handle at any one time. When in stressful situations, I do not return to old coping skills or habits, and my production level is off the charts now. I also treat myself to massages, long walks, quiet time, and exercise when I feel stress in my life. I have a balance in my life among work, play, family, and friends. I allow others input into my life now, so I can share the load. I cannot do it alone. When I thought I had to in the past, that is when my stress level was off the charts. When engaging individuals or situations that in the past brought stress into my life, I have boundaries that keep me grounded. I do this for my well being, no matter what the other person may think of me.

Anger:

Today, when I'm getting angry at myself, at others, or at situations, I step back and ask how I will benefit from being angry. I know that, for me, being angry means I have some type of displeasure with someone or something or myself. My anger in the past showed a lack of communication skills on my part. Today, I know how to communicate my needs to myself and others. I also look at what anger did to me in the past, from self-inflicted physical pain to emotional turmoil that almost took my life on more than one occasion. Anger drains me of emotional and physical energy that can be used productively. And if I do get angry or have a terse word for someone, I am the first to admit I am wrong and apologize for my behavior. The apology does not give me a free pass for what I have done or said. There are consequences. Today, I freely accept my responsibility for anything I do.

Failure:

I do not believe that there is any such thing as failure. What I believe is that there are things we do not accomplish in life, but which we can once we have a foundation that brings about change in our lives. We can see through our choices to success. Whenever I looked at my past, I always thought I was a failure because I could not do simple things, such as pay a bill, hold a job, or sometimes even bathe myself. But it was not that I *could* not do these things – I had certain things missing from my life that would have allowed me to do these things. Now all those components are together in my life and there is really nothing I cannot do. My success lies within my ability to make changes when needed.

Mistakes:

I learned a long time ago that my past mistakes can and will overcome me at any time if I stop trying to find success and solutions each day.

Regrets:

I used to have so many regrets as to the way I lived my life and treated people. It was so overwhelming that I could never make peace with myself or others. Today, I have no regrets. Regrets to me are a waste of energy and time. I asked for forgiveness many times from people and myself for the things I did in my past. Very few even gave me the time of day. I abused myself because I could not forgive *me*. Once I forgave myself, I did not seek others' forgiveness. How they react is their choice, how I react is mine. And self-forgiveness has allowed me to have no regrets.

Exercise:

Today, I view exercise in a completely new light. In my past, I used exercise to control my food intake when I binged too much and to deal with my severe hatred of my body. I no longer panic if I miss a day or a week or even a month at the gym. I know the reason I spent so much time exercising in past was to overcome the distorted thoughts I had about myself and my body as my identity. I do not need someone else's opinion about my body to feel good about *me* anymore. I use exercise to help me feel good about myself, rather than as punishment for over eating or as an instrument of self-hate. When I do eat a little more than I have planned, I do not run to the gym or add exercises to my workout to compensate. I use exercise in my life today for healthy reasons rather than as an obsession. My workouts can be at the gym, home, outside, at a hotel – wherever. There is no set time for me to be at the gym because I do not have the self-hatred I had in the past. I use the gym as a tool in my recovery instead of as the answer to my problems.

Sex:

Today, sex is something I look forword to having with someone with whom I have an emotional connection. And I do not need sex as medicine to deal with issues I come upon in my life. Having a very healthy sex drive in my past led me to use sex as a drug, like most of my dysfunctional thoughts, actions, and behaviors. Since sex was like breathing to me, I abused it because I could do so *so* easily. I had no real idea of the emotional connection between the body and mind when it came to sexual contact. The idea of "making love" – an emotional experience – is a great feeling to look forward to, even though I have never "made love." I do not look at sex as if it is just there for the taking anymore. The physical pleasure it brings is out of this world, but it became numbing to me because I abused it so often.

Relationships:

Today, the connections I have with others are based on honesty and mutual needs, not like in the past when it was all about *me* and my need to victimize others for my lifestyle. There is a quality about my relationships, based on trust, respect, and boundaries, that I never had before. It is a great feeling to know I can have these relationships without second guessing others or myself. My relationships are not moment to moment anymore, with people serving a purpose for my needs. My relationships are continuous and growing each day. In my relationships, I listen and hear what others have to say and offer, not just what I want to say. I am happy to know that I can build solid relationships now without some hidden, selfish reason.

Self-Esteem:

Today I love and like myself more than I ever thought possible, because I learned it was OK to make changes in my life that brought about growth and self-respect. In making changes and taking risks I built up my confidence, without the false hope of my addictions and dysfunctional behaviors. I started liking the fact that I could make things happen, and could hold down a job and pay my bills, eat without binging or purging, be responsible and accountable for myself. It took time but all these little things which turned into big things built up my belief in me. I take pride in myself as a person.

Asking for help:

Today I ask for help when I need it. Asking for help makes me a stronger and better person. It is when I do *not* ask for help that I am weak. Not asking for help kept me shallow and in despair for many years. I have few I trust, but those are the ones I reach out to when I need guidance.

Boundaries:

Today I set limits on myself, other people, and situations in my life. These limits allow me to interact with others without turning to past habits to cope with my needs. In order to start on the path I have walked in my recovery process, one of the most painful things I had to learn was to set boundaries and observe them no matter the outcome. I realized that with boundaries I was only responsible for my "side" and I could not control how others reacted. The boundaries I have in place today make my life a much safer place for me to live in. I have healthy boundaries with family, friends, sex, food, money, work, and everything else I encounter. Remember, *I am an addict* – anything that could help me feel good is something I could go overboard on and then stumble off my path in recovery. But, I am aware of what causes me to stumble – therefore I have boundaries.

I wake up each day and ask myself what I will not tolerate from myself or others, that which does not help my well-being or theirs. This allows me to look at myself and situations and see what is beneficial and what is not. It works for me each day.

Intimacy:

Today, for the first time in my life, I have a complete understanding of intimacy, and it has nothing to do with sexual contact with another person. The sexual act *can* be intimate, but only after the groundwork for emotional intimacy is in place. Intimacy, to me, is that most private moment shared with that someone, a special connection that you have. It is a slight touch of another's arm, looking into another's eyes, holding hands, talking about one's needs and wants with another, sharing who you are with another person, allowing yourself to love no matter the pain from past loves lost. Intimacy is sharing who you are and what you are with another, and that is a great feeling if you can get that feeling with one you love and care about, whether it be family or friend.

Communication skills:

Today I can communicate with others because I no longer make everything about *me*. I am able to hear what others have to say by listening to them. I accept what others have to offer, no matter if I use their help or not. Today, I do not know everything like I thought I did in the past. I am able to learn from others. With these new communication skills, I am able to grow as a person and make changes in my life that lead me in new directions.

Trust:

Today I trust myself to make decisions and choices without fear. I do not let the pain of my past or the bad relationships I had with other people impede my progress today. The confidence I have today is built on my recovery path, with hope that I can overcome those things that led me toward self-destruction for so many years. And I *have* overcome them. I believe in me, and that allows me to believe in others and in life itself. I know that if I make a mistake, I learn from it and go on. I trust that those mistakes – that at times I look forward to making – will lead me to a greater trust in myself and what I do.

Power from within:

Today, I am no longer helpless, as I thought I was in the past. Nor do I act to get sympathy or control of others or of situations. I know that the answers I have always sought are right here within me. Through my recovery program, I have built up an awareness of what it is I have sought in life, and when I step back and out of my own way I see the solutions I seek.

Relapse Prevention:

Today, I set boundaries with myself, situations, and others, so that I do not have a craving or need to go back to the old habits in my life that led to dysfunctional thoughts and behaviors. I can anticipate when these moments may happen, and use the boundaries I have created to get through those moments. I have been able to know where trigger situations may lie and avoid them before they could grab me.

Responsibility:

Today, I have a clear understanding of what is right and wrong in my life. I know when I make a choice that is wrong, and I know that there are consequences. I have an obligation to myself now that I never had before. I can now depend on myself to get things done that, in the past, I would have felt were impossible or unnecessary. I am responsible for *me* and what I do today, no matter the outcome.

Accountability:

Today I take credit for what I do and make amends for my actions if it is necessary. I am the only who can do this for me. *I* pay the price, whatever it may be.

Faith & Spirituality:

In my past, the only faith I had was in my survival skills. Boy, was that a joke. My faith in myself led me to an abyss I would never wish on anyone. I always wanted to be able to see what it was that I should have faith in. It needed to be concrete like the sun and moon, right there for me to see with my own (blind) eyes.

I learned that faith is something I feel within myself, something I feel in my heart and know that it is the right choice at that moment for me. Perhaps that choice does not work out, but it leads me to another choice, and that is what faith is – not letting anything get in the way of my progress.

I do not have to see it to believe in it. I have an understanding now in my faith that allows me to believe without any proof, as with my belief in a higher power I call God. I cannot see Him in front of me as I would another man or woman, but I see Him through the wonders I see each day in children, mountains, people, animals, flowers, the sky, and so much more. My faith allows me to take chances and know that there is something or someone greater than me leading. The serenity that spirituality brings in my life is proof enough that spirituality is God given.

God:

I know that God is in my life each day, because without Him I would have never have begun my journey to recovery. Everything I went through and did in life should have landed me behind bars or six feet under. My God had a purpose for me – to share my story with others so they know they are not alone, and so they can find inside the solutions they seek. I have no regrets at all, and I am able to say this with truth and honesty because my God has forgiven me and allowed me to forgive myself for past – and future – mistakes, which I will make because I am only human. My God knows what I do and accepts my actions, then guides me to solutions after I have exhausted all of my own resources.

Chapter Seventeen: Your Path?

We pick people to surround us who are like us or the people we grew up with, meaning family and friends. I remember so many times while growing up that there were people who told me I would never amount to anything because I did not adhere to their advice or way of life – including my own family and teachers. I did not escape these words of shame and guilt until I was older and said, "To hell with them. I will show them what I can do." And, boy, did I. I went out of my way to prove them right, so I had no need to be responsible and accountable to anything I did. If I was predestined by these so-called loved ones and authority figures, then it was my duty to not let them down.

This was the greatest excuse I could have ever wanted, an excuse I used for years as to why I could not or did not get better. I knew after a short time working this program that I could never get better if I kept thinking that I would stay sick or dysfunctional to show those who hurt me how wrong they were, because in reality I was the only one who suffered. Once I looked at THE NUTRITION & BODY IMAGE PROGRAM™ and what it represented to me, I was able to see clearly how these individuals dealt with their own unhealthy lives by taking them out on me.

Since I knew no better as a child, it was natural for me to live the way they said I would. And with any kind of abuse, if we cannot get the help we need we become the abusers of those weaker than ourselves. I became, as I said, a victimizer. By looking at why I went on the offense with most people I met and needed to get them before they got me, so to speak, I realized that I was acting out to survive and that those tools were not healthy. I did not get anywhere using this type of lifestyle; I was going nowhere faster than a speeding bullet.

What I have learned about myself is the single most important thing I can share with anyone. I learned I had the *right* to be happy and healthy – not a privilege, as some people think. It is a privilege to drive a car, but you and I are not cars. It is our right to seek happiness and a healthy lifestyle, but we have to participate. They will not just come by praying or asking. I learned it was OK to be me for who I am, not what I thought others needed me to be so I would be liked by them. I began to realize that as long as I am compassionate towards others and myself I do not need to worry about what others think about me or my lifestyle – I can respect others' points of view and beliefs but I do not need to make them mine. By treating myself with this new love and respect, I, in turn, treat others the same way.

What a great feeling to know I can do this and not worry, as before, if you the reader or family or friends or people I do not even know think differently about me because of your own points of view and belief systems or lifestyles. The program is what brought me to think like this and opened doors that seemed glued shut all my life. As I have said and will say again, this was not a quick fix for me. It took time – time well spent. Any time you read or hear that your issues and troubles can be over in a short time, look at this offer hard and see if it is just another impossible quick fix.

I learned that honesty is the one thing that is so hard to accept, no matter how hard I try to be honest with myself and others. I know at times I will be judged, shamed, ridiculed, put under a microscope, and have people try and tell me what I feel, believe, think, or do is wrong because I am honest in the way I live. Being honest with myself allowed me the freedom to be honest with others. This can be the same for you as well. I know that many people look at my honesty toward life and even this book and question it. I am perfectly happy that they can do that. It is their right. But my rights and happiness are just as important. This may seem defensive to some, but I really believe that it is right to let others say what they want because we have no real control over what they say and do, but we have control over how we allow others to affect us with their words and actions.

Through the program I have come to understand that, for my personal needs, I have to *work* at my recovery process. I cannot work on my well being for a month and then try to incorporate my past coping skills to see if I will be OK. My past is past and I have left it there. I have not forgotten about it nor will I ever. What I have chosen to do is keep the new boundaries I have created with every aspect of my life, for my best interests. I have met many therapists in the eating disorder field and other addiction fields who tell their clients and the families of their clients that they are cured from all the issues that contributed to their eating disorder problems and other addictions. This gives hope to many. And hope is a great thing. But false hope is a part of the dysfunctional lifestyles which many people still lead. I choose to never say I'm cured from my eating disorder, because many of the issues, situations, people, and experiences that drove me to self-medicate myself are still out there. But the boundaries I have set keep me strong and free of my old lifestyle. Leading by example and honesty are what allow each of us to help or set examples that others can follow.

After many years of trying to find the right ingredients for solutions to my problems, THE NUTRITION & BODY IMAGE PROGRAM™ has allowed me to embrace the success I have in many different aspects of my life and enjoy who I am today. I am sure many of you, at some point in your life, have had someone say that you have the potential for great things. Whether it is school, leadership, a spouse, a career, or whatever, you have the potential to be anything you want, no matter what your religion, race, gender, economic background, or ethnic background. I truly believe this. But the one thing that many of us have done is played off that potential without really working to make the changes in our lives necessary to bring that potential to reality. I have learned that it is not potential that makes us who or what we are, it is our choices that define us. And change is a choice. The reason I mention "potential" is that I have had the potential to do something great all my life, but I always chose the wrong solutions. Now my potential is being fulfilled because I continue to make choices that bring about positive changes in my life. And I learn from each choice I make, whether good or bad. If the choice does not work for me, I do not abuse myself or get angry with myself, I look for a different, positive choice.

Another big step for me was to build enough self-esteem and belief in my choices so that I did not sabotage myself, as I had done in so many instances in my past. Part of building self-esteem was to trust my choices and not to doubt myself every moment of every day. It took time to build trust in my own choices. By learning to trust and believe in myself, I learned that my negative thoughts created negative behaviors and isolation.

I want you to understand that we each have our own process to and through recovery. During my recovery period, I learned that I could not expect understanding from others because my past – which affected so many – was fresh in their memories. I understood that no one had gone through what I had gone through – no one else lived my life. As they did not live it, it was not easy for them to understand my lifestyle and choices. In working on myself I had to learn to be very tolerant of myself and those around me in order for my recovery process to take shape. Today, when I face situations that challenge me, I let others know what I am experiencing. I avoid situations that bring about negative responses that will return me to my old coping skills, but, if I am put in such a situation by others or circumstances out of my control, I have great tools to use to get me through. At the same time, I may not understand someone else's needs. So I ask, and listen if they want to discuss things with me. I create as clear a line of communication as I possibly can with each of the people in my life so that we hear each other and, hopefully, deal with situations as they arise in a healthy and constructive manner.

I have mentioned many tools that THE NUTRITION & BODY IMAGE PROGRAM™ has brought into my life today. Through hard work, I have made it to where I am today and want to share with you how I got here. I have learned how to cope with many situations that, if I had not had my new coping skills, I would have most likely turned to the substance I used to sedate and numb myself before – food.

The first reality I had to deal with in order to see myself and move forward was to understand that I had a problem, accept the truth about myself and everything in my life (I did this with honesty and self-forgiveness), and then take action. It was not easy to admit I was like the person you have read about or did the things I did to myself and others. I felt it was my destiny to live in pain and shame because I was a worthless piece of human waste. But I have never been worthless. I have always been a valuable part of society. I just did not know it or believe it.

Today I live in recovery every moment of every day. As I stated before, I have made the choice never to say to someone that I am cured from my eating disorder and other addictions, because I will always face predicaments that in the past led me to the abyss. The foundation I have today keeps me aware of who and what I am, and allows me freedom of choice, forgiveness, and self-love. With THE NUTRITION & BODY IMAGE PROGRAM™, I have been able to maintain the awareness I need to get through life on an even balance that I had never known before. The more I am aware of what brought about my need to misuse food, sex, and other behaviors, ideas, thoughts, and actions, the better chance I have of never going backwards. And if I did, by some chance, go backwards, then I have the tools to get me back on track – as you can have as well: The Nutrition & Body Image Program™. I need to know that I can do the things I need each day to survive, and I *do* know that because I have a greater understanding and love for Dennis Henning than I ever had.

For more information on *The Daily Process, 16 Points of Life*© and THE NUTRITION & BODY IMAGE PROGRAM™, see
<u>http://www.nutritionbodyimage.com</u>.

Printed in the United States
147446LV00001B/60/A

Dear Reader,

There's a place where life moves a little slower, where a neighborly smile and a friendly hello can still be heard. Where news of a wedding or a baby on the way is a reason to celebrate—and gossip travels faster than a telegram! Where hope lives in the heart, and love's promises last a lifetime.

The year is 1874, and the place is Harmony, Kansas . . .

A TOWN CALLED HARMONY

PASSING FANCY

Suzanna Lind's an expert at farming—and comes to help out her new neighbor, a stuffy Englishman who doesn't know a bushel from a billy goat . . .

Edward Winchester came to Harmony to make his fortune on the Double B farm—and finds it's much harder than it seems in his farming manuals . . .

Reluctantly hiring Zan to show him the ropes, Edward is galled when this sassy tomboy—in a ponytail and men's dungarees, no less—snaps that he'll never be a success at farming. He snaps back that she could never be a real lady like the lovely ladies back home. Zan sets out to prove that she can be a perfect lady—right down to delicate manners and a frilly dress—at the upcoming prairie ball. But underneath their war of words, a growing attraction will soon reveal the true gentleman and lady in each of them . . .

Turn the page to meet the folks of Harmony, Kansas . . .

Welcome to A TOWN CALLED HARMONY . . .

MAISIE HASTINGS & MINNIE PARKER, *proprietors of the boardinghouse* . . . These lively ladies, twins who are both widowed, are competitive to a fault—Who bakes the lightest biscuits? Whose husband was worse? Who can say the most eloquent and (to their boarders' chagrin) the longest grace? And who is the better matchmaker? They'll do almost anything to outdo each other—and absolutely everything to bring loving hearts together!

JAKE SUTHERLAND, *the blacksmith* . . . Amidst the workings of his livery stable, he feels right at home. But when it comes to talking to a lady, Jake is awkward, tongue-tied . . . and positively timid!

JANE CARSON, *the dressmaker* . . . She wanted to be a doctor like her grandfather. But the eccentric old man decided that wasn't a ladylike career—and bought her a dress shop. Jane named it in his honor: You Sew and Sew. She can sew anything, but she'd rather stitch a wound than a hem.

ALEXANDER EVANS, *the newspaperman* . . . He runs *The Harmony Sentinel* with his daughter Samantha, an outspoken, college-educated columnist and certainly Harmony's most fashionable lady. Once, she imagined a sophisticated doctor would be her perfect match—until smooth-talking saloonkeep Cord Spencer worked his way into her heart.

JAMES AND LILLIAN TAYLOR, *owners of the mercantile and post office* . . . With their six children, they're Harmony's wealthiest and most prolific family. It was Lillie, as a member of the Beautification Committee, who acquired the brightly colored paints that brightened the town.

"LUSCIOUS" LOTTIE McGEE, *owner of the First Resort* . . . Lottie's girls sing and dance and even entertain upstairs . . . but Lottie herself is the main attraction at her enticing saloon. And when it comes to taking care of her own cousin, this enticing madam is all maternal instinct.

CORD SPENCER, *owner of the Last Resort* . . . Things sometimes get out of hand at Spencer's rowdy tavern, but he's mostly a good-natured scoundrel who doesn't mean any harm. And when push comes to shove, he'd be the first to put his life on the line for a friend.

SHERIFF TRAVIS MILLER, *the lawman* . . . The townsfolk don't always like the way he bends the law a bit when the saloons need a little straightening up. But Travis Miller listens to only one thing when it comes to deciding on the law: his conscience.

ZEKE GALLAGHER, *the barber and the dentist* . . . When he doesn't have his nose in a dime western, the white-whiskered, blue-eyed Zeke is probably making up stories of his own—*or* flirting with the ladies. But not all his tales are just talk—once he really *was* a notorious gunfighter . . .